ALISON'S DIARY

ALISON'S DIARY

THE NAPPY YEARS

Alison Craig

BLACK & WHITE PUBLISHING

First published 2003
by Black & White Publishing Ltd
99 Giles Street, Edinburgh EH6 6BZ
Reprinted 2003
ISBN 1 902927 98 2

British Library Cataloguing in Publication Data:
A catalogue record for this book is available
from the British Library.

Cover photography: Stephen Kearney
Cover design: Gary Day-Ellison

Printed and bound by Creative Print & Design

For my son, Louis, and mothers everywhere
— especially Pat.
(And with love and thanks to Dave and Eric too
for being great dads!)

FOREWORD

Elaine C. Smith

We've read *Bridget Jones's Diary*, seen the movie, marvelled at Renee Zellwegger's ability to put on and then shed four stone.

Ladies and gentlemen – yes, men will definitely read this, if only because their pregnant partners are standing over them brandishing a sharp object! – ladies and gents, here is a diary – a *real* diary of a *real* woman and her ability to gain four stone then lose it again by producing a bouncing baby at the end! This is what happened to Bridget Jones after she married Mark Darcy and got up the duff!

Alison has done a fantastic job in capturing the fear, anxiety and day-to-day madness that is being pregnant for the first time. Her style does not sensationalise to terrify you as a reader. Instead, it makes you laugh while conveying all the fears you ever had about having your first child.

I wish that I'd had a book like this to read at that very scary time in my life. I simply felt marooned in a little pregnant world of madness that I believed was only inhabited by me! What joy I would have felt had I known that so many of the pregnant women I saw and who appeared to be coping brilliantly were feeling just as terrified and out of control as I was! All those women who 'bloomed' during pregnancy, who didn't get purple and breathless at the top of the stairs, who had two days of slight nausea and then nothing, who gained the exact amount of weight they were supposed to and were then back at step aerobics a month after the birth and who never seemed to want to kill their husbands for simply not being pregnant. If only I had known that I was not alone and that all these women felt marooned on that little island of pregnancy as well, then we could have met up and had parties, drunk on the madness of each other's raging hormones.

I'm glad to say that this book brings comfort and joy where it's needed most. Parenthood is a very scary thing and even scarier for women who have had careers and a great deal of control over their own lives. Hence, the desire to control the pregnancy and the birth. The problems arise when you realise that you can't control anything about the process anymore . . . not even when you need to pee. You've got to go when you've got to go!

There's some comfort in the knowledge that most of us survive the whole process with a few brain cells still intact, and certainly by the second and third pregnancies the shock decreases – although different fears arise. We don't like to tempt fate and so worry that, just because we got through the first one with a healthy outcome, it doesn't mean that the next will go smoothly too. But generally our anxieties are never as high as for the first time around. Our fears about being parents and doing the right thing lessen and, by the time you have three kids, you let them juggle knives without batting an eyelid, saying, 'Well done, darling, how clever!' – whereas the first one was rushed off to the Sick Kids' Casualty Department even if they just fell off their bike.

I recommend this book to everyone.

If you're pregnant for the first time, then you'll find great solace in the fact that you're not alone and will laugh out loud at the truths and similarities to your own experience. If it's your second or subsequent pregnancy, read and remember . . . and then think about being stupid enough to go through it all *again!*

If you're a man, read it because *you just bloody should and try to learn something about pain and suffering!*

And if you're in your forties like me and consider that this part of your life is done and dusted, then just sit back and enjoy this very fact – looking superior, wise and full of wisdom . . . and maybe with a slight gloating smirk on the lips.

Enjoy!

INTRODUCTION

I was thirty-one when I had my son, Louis, and at the time I thought I knew it all. This was not going to faze me. I wouldn't put on any excess weight during pregnancy, I'd remain calm and in control and, of course, I'd be back at work within days of giving birth. It was not going to change my life.

Huh! Naturally, when theory gave way to reality, my world turned upside down.

Why didn't anyone tell me? Why did no one warn me? Would I have listened? No, you're right. Probably not.

Each book and pamphlet I found showed clean, serene, perky-looking women with normal sized breasts that defied gravity, wearing size 8 jeans and smiling as they cradled their newborn children. Which begged the question: what the hell was wrong with me that I was fourteen-and-a-half stone, had breasts the size of Austria and was utterly exhausted and scared out of my wits at the prospect of being left alone with a baby and with absolutely no idea how to look after him?

The conclusion? I was not normal.

As time has passed I have realised that my experience is far from unique and yet – incredibly, in the new millennium – the real truth about pregnancy, birth and motherhood is still the best-kept secret in the world.

So here is my personal diary of that time in my life. It's a truthful account of how it was for me – an average woman of average weight and average expectation. And if it makes just one woman feel better about their own hormonal fluctuations, wobbly bottom and insecurities as they embark on the great adventure of being a parent, then hallelujah!

Alison Craig

ALISON'S DIARY

17 March
10 stone

Speak to my friend Elaine on the phone, who tells me she's pregnant. 'God, how did you know?' I ask, and so she goes through her symptoms, one by one. Most of them I seem to suffer from permanently, I joke, as she lists irritability, peeing all the time, tiredness and emotional outbursts. But then I hear her say, 'Oh . . . and my nipples! They stick out so far you could hang a coat on them.' With a gulp, I glance down at my denim jacket – which is, coincidentally, hanging from one of my nipples – say bye and slam down the phone. Mmmm. I know I'm not that regular, but surely not.

Run to the chemist, shuffle around and blush furiously whilst buying a pregnancy test. Thunder home, get the stick out of the packet and read the instructions. Just as a precaution, I decide to do the test – having by now convinced myself it's not the case. I can't be pregnant. Hands shaking so violently that I not only pee on the stick but on my arm, sleeve and hand as well.

Have a shower whilst waiting for the test to develop. By the time I get out, the test is positive. Hands really shaking now. Clamp the instruction leaflet firmly with both to stop it flapping around and reread it. Ah, so it was only supposed to be left for *three* minutes. As the shower took eight, it's most likely wrong.

Walk back to the chemist in a casual way. I mean, I can't be running around like a ferret if I'm pregnant – which obviously I'm not, but anyway. Convinced the pharmacist smirks at me.

Heart rate dangerously high as I open the second test. This time am careful with my aim. Dry arm and hand but wet face. Same result. The blue line appears, shortly followed by the tears. Holy shit, I'm up the duff.

Due at a meeting at the radio station at 4 p.m. Dress carefully, put on my make-up and set off. Utterly convinced everyone will know just by looking at me that I'm with child. I AM WITH CHILD. The meeting's to talk about an outside broadcast we're doing from Berlin in a month. There are general gales of laughter, lederhosen jokes and endless references to beer. For once I sit back, which may explain the number of times I'm asked, 'Alison, are you all right?'

I sit, smile wanly and nod. 'Yes, I'm fine. Why?' I know that they know.

' 'Cos you're usually bossing everyone around and you've hardly said a word,' says my co-presenter, John.

'Bugger off!' I reply.

'Yeah, she's OK. She's obviously got a hangover,' says someone else as the meeting resumes and banter continues to fly round the table. There's little point in my being there as I've no idea what's going on. I can't stop thinking about what's happening in my tummy. A baby, a bairn, a wee thing is alive within my beer belly. Help!

7 p.m.

Hastily arrange to meet my husband David and break the news. No idea how to do it. Think, 'I'm a mature woman, it'll be easy.' It's not. He's immediately suspicious when I order a lime and soda, wondering why I'm not horsing down my usual pint of lager. I brush it off saying I'm thirsty.

We order food and start talking about the house which we're renovating at the moment. He tells me we can't get a council grant to take the lead piping out unless we've someone in the house who's pregnant.

'Oh well!' I say, 'we'll get that grant then.' It shows how little he listens to me 'cos it's only after I reiterate my subtle little point three times that the penny finally drops, his jaw drops and my self-confidence drops with it. I start crying. God, my hormones have obviously started rampaging early.

We talk about it and I can see he's as shocked as I am. It's not that we didn't plan to have a baby. Well, actually we didn't plan anything. We didn't really talk about it at all. We both sort of assumed that we would – one day – and sort of left it at that. He's busy having just started his restaurant and I'm doing a radio show six days a week, so I guess it just never crossed our minds that this would in fact be the day.

We toast our wonderful news and go home to be shocked in our flat.

18 March
4.30 a.m.

Awake most of the night worrying. You see, four weeks ago we put a bid in for that house and didn't think we'd get it. Shockingly, we did and now we have to renovate the entire thing from top to bottom. This bit doesn't bother me. The problem is what happened after we got the house. Dave and I agreed that, once we'd paid for everything, we'd never have enough money to have another holiday ever again. So, on a whim, that very same day we went to a travel agent and got last-minute flights to Gran Canaria for £49. We left from Edinburgh the following day.

We had no accommodation organised, but that didn't matter, I said, 'We'll be happy anywhere.' As it was, we ended up in a scuzzy wee room on foam mattresses above a club in Puerto Rico.

When I'd said 'happy anywhere', clearly I was lying. It was so hot and noisy that the only way we could get any sleep was to drink heavily until we could be guaranteed to collapse into a deep coma, which would last until the club downstairs shut up shop at 4 a.m. At this point, the peace and quiet would wake us up and we'd take it in turns to stumble around looking for water to glug before retiring once more to our itchy, sandy, foam hell for some more fitful kip. This was our routine, apart from the night we met a charming South African guy who lived in a cave and who, after we'd bemoaned the sweat box we were lumbered with, offered to put us up for the night. He seemed very down to earth, so we accepted gratefully and followed him up a few back alleys – where we ended up lying on a itchy, sandy *cave* floor for a change. It was so rough I remember being homesick for our hell-hole. In the morning Dave gave our host his Doc Martens by way of thanks, as the guy's trainers only had one sole.

What I suppose I'm trying to say is that, no matter which way you look at it, we did not experience a week of temperance and good behaviour while away on holiday. In fact, when I think of it, I'm fairly sure not one piece of fruit nor a single vegetable were consumed by yours truly. So, after that week of shocking behaviour, we then flew home . . . and carried on partying. We had to. The day after we returned, we got the keys to the new house!

With our livers barely dry, we invited some pals round to celebrate amongst the rubble and smell of old man's urine. Loads of bottles of wine and fun later, we got a taxi back to our old flat and suffered the inevitable consequences the next day. Hey, there was nothing to worry about! We were young and carefree. At least, that was what I thought. With a sickening feeling in my tummy, it now dawns on me that, during the entire time – during the excesses of Gran Canaria and the subsequent celebrations at home – I was pregnant. There was a baby in my tummy. A completely dependant little dot of a human relying on me to nurture it. And what was I doing? *Oh – my – God*. What have I done?

9 a.m.

Standing outside Waterstone's bookshop waiting for it to open so I can buy a book about pregnancy and babies. I don't know anything about it. I mean, absolutely nothing – other than the nipple thing, obviously. I need to find out what's going to happen and what the past five weeks of my life may have done to the unsuspecting foetus.

The baby section is huge. There are so many different manuals, encyclopaedias, tips for this and tips for that. Where in God's name do I start? After a good browse, I plump for Dr Miriam Stoppard's *Complete Guide to Conception,* – well, we can tear that section out – *Pregnancy and Birth.* It's a big book with lots of large, coloured photographs and diagrams. This is what I need, the idiot's guide to pregnancy. All I want to do now is go home and read it from cover to cover, but I must go to work. My radio show starts at midday and it's now 10.30 a.m., so I buy a copy of *The Times* as well and wrap Dr Miriam inside it. I don't want anyone to know yet.

11 a.m.

I should've known better. No sooner am I in the door of the radio station than Maureen – the lovely receptionist – clocks *The Times* and says, 'Oh, you've gone all up market! What are you doing reading that rubbish?'

Blushing furiously, I mutter something about there being a very interesting article in it on Madonna – which seems unlikely, but goes some way towards explaining what I'm doing in possession of a broadsheet newspaper – so she smiles and let's me pass without any further questioning. God, I feel like a criminal hiding something terrible in my bag. A shop-lifter or a pervert with some dirty mag stashed in there.

Heart thumping, I make it to the fourth floor by foot and exhale as I sit at my desk. The place looks deserted, so I tentatively slip Dr Miriam's book out on to my desk. Just as I open it, I hear the booming voice of one of the other DJs.

'Hey, Ali Bally,' – I *hate* being called Ali Bally – 'how's it hanging?'

Dr Miriam is snapped shut, pushed back into *The Times* and shoved into a drawer as the most irritating man in the world perches his left buttock on the corner of my desk and proceeds to relive every moment of his radio show for the benefit of no one but himself as I'm sure no other eejit could bear to listen to it anyway. It seems I'll have to wait till later. Damn.

5 p.m.

Can't wait to get home and read my book in private. First thing I do is run a bath. I get in. Prod my tummy. Get out. Stand side-on to the mirror. Don't think I can see any difference. Admittedly, it's hard to tell, since I've never been of the bony variety. My bum's certainly huge, but then it has been for years.

Open the book and, the next thing I know, Dave's waking me up. Waking me up? Is this another symptom, dozing off like an old wifie in the early evening? Dave cooks us supper – yes, he's a chef and yes, he's a doting father-to-be. This could work out very well for me and the person within. I go to bed early. Must be a combination of shock and guilt that's making me so tired. It's been such a long day.

19 March

Lie in bed reading Dr M. Blimey! There's a lot to take in. Long lists of dos and don'ts. The two main ones jump out at me and worry me sick – don't smoke and don't drink alcohol. Well, there are my two favourite pastimes off the cards then.

'Actually,' I say to Dave, who's trying to sleep next to me, 'the thought of a fag repulses me. Yuk! Drinking too.' At which point he wakes up enough to point out that it's only 7.30 a.m. Fair point.

First thing I must do is make an appointment with my doctor to ask 10,000 questions and have things confirmed.

20 March

The doctor does a quick test and then, after asking me a few questions, confirms that I am, in fact, with child. It's due around 17 November, plus or minus five days, by all accounts.

After the initial chat, I eventually pluck up the courage to ask the question that has been haunting me since I found out. Yes – the one about our wild week in Gran Canaria. Could any living being have survived the amount of abuse that I unwittingly levelled at it during my holiday? When pressed by the doc, I dilute the actual consumption rate by about half, but even on this basis his eyebrows raise and he admits, 'Yes, that is rather a lot to drink.' Guilt is coursing through me, so I confess I've been a bit economical with the truth. His eyebrows almost leave his forehead when I give him a brief synopsis of our trip. Bless him, he does put my mind at rest when he tells me most people don't realise they're pregnant till about this time and that my lifestyle is not unique. In his experience, as long as I'm good from here on in there should be nothing to worry about. Phew!

Just as I'm about to leave, though, I do ask him how experienced he is *exactly*. Twenty-five years. I relax a little for the first time.

8.30 p.m.

Out to friends for dinner tonight. It's a murder-mystery party. We've decided not to tell anyone till I'm twelve weeks pregnant. It's our secret and bloody hard to keep, especially as I'm not known for making one glass of wine last the whole evening. Tonight, though, I'm dressed as an air hostess, Dave as a mad count, my cousin's husband in a ski suit, and the other guests look equally bizarre so there are lots of other distractions. No one notices. It's strange – I must look the same, as no one says anything. I just feel so different, so changed.

Sadly, the thought of smoking and drinking is not repelling David – a.k.a. LSH or Long-Suffering Husband – who's carrying on as if everything is normal. Everything is *not* normal. I've a human being in my belly. I feel sick and I feel tired. Everything is different. How can he do this?

21 March

Watch with interest as hangover unfurls. Dave awakes to find me sitting bolt upright reading Dr M's book as he opens a red eye. I begin by reading him a few interesting facts before showing him a picture of a woman in childbirth. That'll teach him.

Almost as soon as I have my condition confirmed by a grown-up doctor in a white coat, I develop morning sickness. Is it psychological? It seems like an awful coincidence. I've watched so many films and TV series over the years where one moment the woman finds out she's having a baby and the next, she's running to the loo to hang her head over the pan. Perhaps I've just subconsciously transformed into a stereotypical mother-to-be? I wonder whether, if I didn't know that I was pregnant, I'd be feeling sick?

Actually, it's irrelevant because, whether it's in my mind or not, all I know is that when I wake up – even before I open my eyes – it's 'Good morning nausea!' The good thing is that morning sickness, it turns out, doesn't necessarily mean spending just the a.m. hours of the day with your head in a toilet. No, it can just be this constant feeling that you're about to throw up, although in fact you don't. Did I say 'the good thing'? OK, it's not ideal, but I can live with it if you can tell me what I can do to stop it? Eat crackers, I'm informed.

22 March

So I eat crackers – still feel nauseous, though. And it might just be hormonal, but the side-effect of downing endless supplies of Ryvita with sesame seeds – the others are too reminiscent of carpet tiles for my liking – seems to be flatulence. Oh dear.

23 March

Friend Sarah's birthday. Everyone out for a meal. She has a lovely wee baby, Ciara, and is eyeing me suspiciously as I sip one glass of wine and look yellow whilst muttering, 'Och, no, I just fancy driving.' She's pregnant with her second child and must notice that all previous conversations about babies had me in the latter stages of boredom whereas now I'm sitting on the edge of my seat, listening to every word, ears pricked for any information that may come in handy. I'm fairly sure she knows, but she doesn't say a word.

Week 6

26 March

Try not to make mention of the sickness at work. My face gives the game away, though, as it's usually white or sometimes, by way of contrast, yellow. Maureen and the others who like to hang about reception gossiping always laugh at me and ask, 'So where were you last night then?' under the illusion that I've been dancing the night away with whichever groovy rock star's in town at the moment. God, if only they knew. That renegade party chick is gone and, in her place, is Alison, regular attendee of the local vomitarium. How they'll laugh when I tell them – but not yet. Although I don't like to dwell on these things, apparently there's a high incidence of miscarriage in the first twelve weeks and I'm only six weeks pregnant. I've only known for a week and it already feels like a lifetime. Forty weeks of this and I'll be insane.

27 March

Battle on with the sick feeling. Now on a packet of crackers a day.

Am on the phone to my chum Elaine, who's a few weeks ahead of me, bemoaning the constant feeling of wanting to barf, and she suggests I try ginger. When I mention this to my loving husband, David's out of the house like a shot procuring the stuff: root ginger, ginger beer, even ginger jam – in fact, anything with ginger in it, just to steer me away from the crackers. He claims it's cruelty to husbands, me sitting around farting like a dray horse. I tell him I can't help it and that it's probably the baby taking after its father.

28 March

The ginger has helped although, when LSH isn't looking, I stuff a quick Ryvita into my chops too. I keep a packet under my side of the bed in case of emergency.

29 March

Popping into the new house every few days. Still waiting for the building warrant. Decide we must get on and do something. I buy some Nitromors and a scraper to make a start on the hall. For some reason the entire house was painted dark brown and it has to be stripped.

As I stand there in my shiny blue paper jumpsuit with a mask over my mouth and a scraper in my hand, Dave comes in and tells me to 'Stop!' Apparently, none of the materials I'm using should be in the hands of the pregnant! So what can I do, eh?

Nothing. No lifting, no moving, no stripping – in more ways than one for fear of unpleasant reaction – so the renovation of the house will be left up to one Mr David Howie Scott and his platoon of workmen. This news does not break my heart.

30 March

Have read Dr M's book from cover to cover. Actually, I wish I hadn't. I'm already fatter than the photograph of the woman who's about five months pregnant. Mind you, I had a head start. She was a stick-thin model before she started, unlike myself. According to the book, I won't be showing yet. Right. My weight is therefore either water retention to end all extreme forms of water retention, or I'm having twins.

Gulp. I suddenly remember that my father had twin brothers, one of whom died at birth. And don't twins run in David's family too? Help! The sooner I have a scan the better. It's not booked in till the beginning of May. I wonder if they would bring it forward.

Week 7

31 March

Doctor says they can't bring the scan forward and I'll have to wait. Hrumph!

1 April

Finally crack and tell a few close friends I'm having a baby. One of them slaps me on the back and says, 'Yeh right! Good one, Alison. I know it's the first of April!' I hadn't even registered but it really is April Fool's Day. Typical. When they see tears welling up in my eyes, they stop the joking.

We'd been to the theatre but I'd waited till we were in the pub afterwards before I'd made my announcement. The girls already knew. They did. They'd all guessed. How? Apparently, I'd asked for an ice cream during the interval while they all snorkled into the gin. Their antennae were immediately up, then Naomi (private eye in the making) clocked that I'm wearing a pair of men's 34-inch-waist trousers with the top button undone and she knew. She spread the word and soon I was the talk of the town. Huh.

Anyway, I'm the first of all our lot to fall pregnant. They don't know what to do. Neither do I. We're not a huggy-kissy lot, so after they say congratulations I go home early to stare at my stomach and eat more ice cream. I think we all sense it. Things are about to change forever.

6. April
10 stone 12 pounds

Am now convinced it's twins. I'm already wearing Dave's jeans. Mine have all failed me. Terrible, lumbering, fat feeling and I'm only a few weeks pregnant. I suspect I'll not be offering the small designer bump look. It's strange but, the moment my nausea abates, all I want to do is stuff my face. I mean, really horse into anything I can get my hands on. Apart from crisps. They repel me. If you'd told me that one day I'd turn my nose up at a box of Walkers salt and vinegar crisps and chew on a piece of root ginger instead, I'd have laughed in your face. Not now. I'm a different woman.

Week 8

7 April

Can't help myself. Have bought a book on twins. Hope it's just one in there.

Week 9

19 April

Dad's birthday. My folks are down from Aberdeen for the night. Dad is speaking at a dinner and is pacing up and down pretending not to be nervous. This presents the ideal opportunity to tell him and Mum that their daughter's pregnant.

Want David to be there at the time, so wait for him to come in. He arrives back late from work with little time to spare. Immediately disappears into the quagmire that is our bedroom and can't find his posh white shirt. I dig it out of the washing machine and he puts it on – wet. It looks fine to me, but Mum tells him to take it off so that she can iron it dry. She spoils him, if you ask me. Still, she irons it dry as he digs around looking for his kilt and the rest of his stuff. There's no time to break our monumental news. I'm livid.

Ten minutes later he's ready to go and off he strides with a big grin on his face – until I call him back and tell him that if he tells my father we're having a baby without me being there I'll kill him. He leaves with less of a grin on his face, knowing that once he's had a few beers he'd better watch his loose tongue, because he can see by the mad, hormonal look in my eye that I'm not joking.

20 April
2.30 a.m.

I can only assume that the tactic David chose to keep his mouth shut last night was to drink too much, too quickly. In such cases, the ability to be coherent at any level whatsoever is negligible. Judging by the racket of doors slamming and suppressed giggling on the communal stair, he took his task seriously and it was successful.

10.30 a.m.

David and Dad are terribly hungover. They can't really function at all. I've had a completely sleepless night as David's snoring reached monumental proportions. My revenge? I eat a few Ryvitas in the middle of the night so that I can torture him during the day when he's feeling less than fragrant.

Eyeing up the two men of the family, I cook them breakfast, which they can't even eat. I look at Mum – who rolls her eyes. She's witnessed such scenes for far longer than I have and takes it in her stride.

Eventually I can't wait one more moment so blurt it out whilst giving Dad the disapproving eye.

'Your behaviour will have to change now you're going to be a grandpa,' I declare.

My dad looks at me and, not understanding one word of what I've just said, immediately changes the subject to golf. As I listen to the conversation, I feel a burning sensation behind my eyes and have difficulty breathing properly. In my head I'm saying, 'Alison, you're a thirty-one-year-old professional woman. Get a grip.' But, try as I might, I can't keep it all in so I burst out crying and run to my room for some expert and histrionic sobbing. I can't help it.

My poor sheepish dad appears at the bedroom door, scared half to death and not knowing what on earth to do with his giant, snottering, pregnant child. However, a quick cuddle from the man who'll never just be a dad again but is now to be a grandpa, and all is well. I soon pick myself up, revert to my adult behaviour pattern and life goes on.

Week 10

22 April

Sickness seems better today. Hallelujah! Perhaps I'm over the worst of it.

23 April

Take the step of putting all ginger products on to a high shelf. If I never taste the stuff again, it'll be too soon. Problem is I'm now so tired I can barely keep my eyes open during the day. For some strange reason I perk up at about 10 p.m., but during the day I could put my head down on any available surface and drop off. David suggests it's because I haven't had a drink or a cigarette for weeks. Dr M, however, says it's quite normal in the first three months.

25 April

At last the sickness has completely gone but – annoyingly – the grumpiness has remained. (Some would say – those who get the sticky end of my pineapple – it's even got worse. Bugger them!)

A skinny eejit of a bloke at work tells me I'm getting fat. What a bloody charmer! I tell him he's got a very small penis, but at least I can lose weight. Nice to know my brain still works occasionally.

Week 11

29 April

Get the building warrant through for the house. Work can start in earnest now. The builders promise they'll have completed the majority of the work by the end of July so that we can move in and get settled before the baby arrives. Then all we need to do is the decoration, painting and so on – i.e. the fun bit! Hormonally start planning the nursery.

Week 12

5 May

Go for my twelve-week scan. Was made to drink loads of water so that they can use the ultrasound machine. I lie down on the bed and they smear clear jelly over my tummy, run this wand across and, all of a sudden, there it is on the TV screen right next to us. An actual baby. *Our* wee baby. Dave and I stare open-mouthed at it. Well, it's true then, there's definitely only one in there. It's absolutely tiny. What I can't understand is that, as soon as I see the wee squirming thing, I've an over-whelming feeling that it's a boy. I just know. Sounds daft, but I do.

'Well, you've got a fifty–fifty chance of being right,' says Mr Romantic.

The good thing is I know it's not just fat now, which is a hell of a relief. I mention this to the midwife, who tells me the baby is now approximately 9 cm long and weighs $1\frac{1}{2}$ oz. So how come I've put on about a stone? She doesn't answer. Probably just as well.

It's amazing to see the wee peanut-shaped person in my tummy. Blimey. I must now be serene and in control and nurture the small thing within. We're parents and we even have a little, grainy, black-and-white photograph to prove it. Now we can tell the whole world!

7 May

Everything has been good, calm and normal for a few days. It can't last, of course. My radio show goes on for a total of three hours. The car park at the radio station is virtually non-existent so there is the daily challenge of 'not getting a parking ticket' – which, in central Edinburgh, is no mean feat. After years of honing my skills in this area, I've got it down to a fine art. First step is to put on a long record – in this case Bruce Springsteen's 'Streets of Philadelphia' at five minutes and ten seconds – to give me the maximum time to rush up to street level from the studio in the basement, run through reception, head for the pay-and-display machine and stuff some change into it, before rushing over to stick the ticket on the car windscreen. The excitement really starts when, with one eye on the clock, you realise you only have thirty seconds left to get back to the studio before the record ends and still have enough breath to open the mike and talk casually to the listeners.

Recently, though, the hormonal swirls within are slowing me up and I cannot believe my eyes today when I spot an evil traffic warden giving me a ticket. I'm a minute over the allotted time. Waving my new ticket to prove my good intentions, I beg her to stop writing the ticket and she completely ignores me. I change tack and grovel for a moment, but she continues to blank me completely. So I just lose it. Suddenly I'm possessed by a screeching banshee who squawks at full volume, 'Just 'cos you're a premenstrual bitch who hasn't had a shag in ten years, there's no need to take it out on me!', before stomping off in high dudgeon. I get back into the studio, very out of breath and highly stressed, with five seconds to spare before the record finishes. I open the microphone and, wheezingly, spout out a hideously unprofessional diatribe about the traffic warden.

3 p.m.
Off air and Boss summons me to his office. I'm duly bollocked out.

8 May
Official complaint has been made against me to the Radio Authority about my outburst. Shit. Carpeted once again. Hang head very low and snuffle. Boss in shock. Pre-pregnant Alison would have ranted and raved till he relented, and I have to say I can't believe it myself when the bloody tears start streaming down my face. Neither of us know what to do so I just leave.

9 May
Decide to tell Boss I'm pregnant. It's not fair. I'm sure he thinks I've lost the plot and as a result will probably sack me if I don't come clean. I admit my moods are quite erratic. I tell him and he bursts out laughing, saying he's relieved I'm not actually turning into an axe murderer. I burst out crying, which soon wipes the smile off his face. Typical bloke – useless in these situations. He gives me a cursory pat on the back in a sort of 'well done' way and then coughs as I dry up my snottery face and make my way down to the studio to start the programme.

10 May
From today onwards I shall adopt a more Jane Asher approach to life. After all, I am a woman too. Henceforth, I'll attempt to embrace a more '50s' housewife attitude to being pregnant – minus the pinny, obviously. I smile sweetly to people and pretend

the diatribe at the traffic warden didn't happen. Think I'm convincing, though I'm perturbed to note there's a definite look of ill-disguised terror in the whites of people's eyes as they nod and smile back at me. They'd better not be pacifying me just 'cos I'm with child or they'll get a thick ear pronto! Oops, my Jane Asher façade seems to have slipped already.

Week 13

13 May

Pelvic floor. What *is* that? Something to do with Elvis Presley? Elvis the Pelvic Floor? Not sure what it's all about, but am told to go to the loo and, in the middle of peeing, to stop myself by doing some sort of internal clench. Try it. It works. So this must be my pelvic floor. Hello.

I've had enough trouble over the years getting motivated to keep the muscles in my outer body in shape, so how exactly I'm expected to suddenly start exercising the ones I didn't even know existed until ten minutes ago is a mystery to me. Although I have seen a guy at the Edinburgh Festival weight-lifting with his genitals. Is that the idea? You get your internal muscles into such tip-top condition that perhaps, if your original career goes by the wayside, there's always a possibility of setting yourself up as a vaguely amusing Fringe act. Clench.

Week 14

19 May

The Jane Asher thing is just not working. I'm not serene, I'm Mrs Angry. Everyone and everything is getting up my nose. Probably because my nose is the only part of my body that hasn't changed shape. Dr M says I could be quite big now or not showing at all. Well, guess which I am. Gi-bloody-normous.

It's our third anniversary today. Out we go for dinner – which is lovely – and then I've the utter joy of being dragged to the pub where there are just clouds of smoke, beer smells and nowhere to sit down. Happy bloody anniversary.

Week 15

27 May
11 stone 8 pounds

Can't stop eating. I mean, I really can't. I'm absolutely ravenous. People say you shouldn't eat for two. That's OK, I'm not. I'm eating for six. Humungous belly. Have been told by doctor to stop eating so much as the scales are way over what they should be. 'Bugger off!' was on the tip of my tongue, but I thought better of it as I went straight from the surgery to the local shop for a Twix and a packet of Joosters. What the hell am I supposed to do? I can't swill wine – a fact my friends seem to have taken a little too literally, as I've been dropped like a steaming turd from the social circle. It seems they don't want me now I've stopped jumping on tables, telling jokes and falling over. Not fair.

28 May

Phone my pal and accuse her of dropping me like the afore-mentioned hot effluence 'cos I can't drink anymore. She denies it. I press her for the truth and I get it. It seems I've been a grumpy sod to my pals too and they don't know what to do with a large Pillsbury Dough girl who bites their heads off. Oh. Wish I hadn't asked now.

Week 16:

8 June

Sister-in-law Kirsty has had a baby. A little girl. They've called her Amy. Off to the hospital to see her. She's beautiful.

'What's it like?' I ask.

'Wonderful,' she says, smiling at her wee bundle of joy. Mmmm.

Phone my cousin Patricia and ask her, 'Is having a baby that sore?'

'Och, no,' she says, 'it just feels like very bad constipation.' Mmmm. I decide I'll ask her that again when I can see her face and check to see if her fingers are crossed behind her back. I'm suspicious there's a conspiracy to veil the truth from the uninitiated. We shall see.

Week 17

11 June
9 p.m.

Lying in bed I feel a very strange, fluttering sensation in my tummy. Initially I think, 'Och, not indigestion – *again*!' But when it doesn't stop for a few minutes, I realise it must be the baby. Aaargh!

Tell Dave, who spends an hour with his hand and ear permanently attached to my tum . . . and feels nothing.

Week 18

19 June
9.30 p.m.

Fluttering feeling again. I call out to Dave, who comes bombing over, jumps on the bed and puts his hand on my tummy. He still doesn't feel it. Must be so small that it can only be felt by me.

21 June

When Dave comes in, he looks very stressed. The new house isn't nearly finished and we must move into it in about two weeks. We've sold the flat and we have to move out. There's no choice. We'll be living in the shed at the bottom of the garden by the sound of things. God. Decide not to dwell on the swatches for the nursery curtains as we may just need an orange crate and a couple of blankets at this rate.

Week 20

23 June

The halfway mark!

According to Dr M I should be feeling well. Correct.

Have more energy than I've had in a while. Correct.

The baby's hearing will have developed to the extent that he'll be able to distinguish different sounds. Right, that's it!

I burst in to see my boss, delighted to have a legitimate reason never to play any more dance music on my programme ever again. I can't play that endless, mindless, repetitive rubbish to my unborn child, I argue. When I inform him I'll be playing a mixture of reggae and AOR, he scratches his beard and – I'm most disturbed to notice – looks a little afraid. Even the boss who can carpet a person at 500 yards is shrinking away from my hormones. God, maybe I should ask for a pay rise.

24 June

Go up to see the house. House? Huh! Shack is more like it. It's got an exterior wall and that's it. There are no insides at all! No walls, no floorboards, no doors, no nothing.

The workmen smile at me in a 'Here comes Mrs Doubtfire' sort of way, presumably thinking I must be jolly 'cos I'm fat. Their illusion is soon dispelled during a two-minute diatribe, which loses its gravity somewhat when I start to cry. Crying in front of all the workmen in our house – what has become of me? The gallant foreman tentatively steps forward and offers me a four-finger Kit Kat. Through my teary eyes I can see he's a nice bloke – a fact confirmed when I notice that his tummy is about the same size as mine – so we call a truce. By the time I leave, the workmen – my new friends Gordon, Brian, Lee and Mark – have promised, on various members of their families' lives, that they'll be finished in our house by the end of July. Unfortunately, we have to move on the 4th, but I'm sure I can handle them and it is only for a couple of weeks.

25 June
12 stone

A friend brings me some lemon oil to rub on my tummy to stop me getting stretch marks. Start liberally applying it. It smells revolting and it's blooming hard to get your clothes on without ending up looking like you've had a bottle of Crisp 'n' Dry poured over you. Still, it'll be worth it. Stretch-mark free – fingers crossed.

26: June

Friend Anne comes up from London with a huge bag of clothes for me from Portobello Market. Lovely. I open it up in great anticipation of having something I can wear that doesn't belong to my 6-foot 14-stone husband. I try to hide my deep disappointment when I discover that the bag is packed to the gunnels with several hideous, oversized, brightly coloured and truly ghastly batik shirts. No one – pregnant, sober, sane or, for that matter, alive – would be seen dead in these, if you see what I mean. I don't mention this as I thank her as best I can, don one over my Demis Roussos shape and smile wanly before heading to bed. It was a lovely thought.

27 June
3 a.m.

Wake up to hear cackling and snorts of laughter as Anne and Dave sit drinking, smoking and laughing their heads off. Look out the bedroom window and there they are, having a great bloody time the way I used to. Livid.

28 June

David's birthday. Can't believe I go out for dinner in a batik shirt.

We both eat and he drinks enough for both of us. I never want to drink again after this is over. I can't believe that sane, lucid, intelligent human beings turn into such loud-mouthed prats that know it all. LSH says it's my hormones. I tell him it's not my bloody hormones and if he says that again I'll stick my fish knife into his throat. I reluctantly acknowledge he may have a point.

Week 21

3 July

Tomorrow we move into our new house. I've deliberately avoided the house since my last outburst as I don't want to scare the men by crying again – plus they promised to have it almost done. So you can imagine my utter horror to find out there's only one room finished.

Our last night in the flat consists of me generally clinging to the banisters crying, 'I don't want to go. You can't make me leave,' and David cajoling me by suggesting we go for a curry to cheer me up. Over my chicken dhansak he talks me down. The facts are that we have no choice other than to bite the bullet and move tomorrow – 'Unless,' he jokes, 'you want to live with the new owners of our flat.' He looks at me sternly. 'No, Alison, you are *not* going to live with them.' I know when I'm beaten. Damn.

4 July

The removal van arrives on schedule and all our furniture is duly taken out and driven away to be put into storage – apart from our bed, a chest of drawers and a telly. I go to work with a heavy heart as well as a heavy body, dreading home time.

5 p.m.

Two hours after my show, I'm still hanging around the office until I can avoid it no longer. I drive to the new house via the old flat just to check that the new owners really have moved in. In my heart, I hope they've had second thoughts and have decided not to bother.

Still with this flicker of hope, I park the car. My heart sinks when I see that the lights are on and they're in. Surreptitiously,

I watch as they bustle about unpacking and placing their belongings. After a few moments they stop and stand in the big bay window admiring the amazing views over the Firth of Forth. They're each holding a glass of wine, their heads move together, they kiss and clink glasses. Toasting their new home – the place that was our home, where we lived happily for the past four years; the place where we first stayed together; the place where we had wild parties and great laughs; the place where we rented out the spare room to three Italian students, pretending we were married so that we could get lots of money from the language school. The façade lasted two days, until I confessed we were charlatans and gave them money to go to McDonald's every night to keep them quiet. It wasn't till they'd long gone that the phone bill arrived and we realised that the moment we left the flat every morning they'd been on the phone to their boyfriends back in Roma for hours! Happy days? Well, certainly wild and crazy. *And*, as I look up at the window with a tear in my eye, undeniably over.

After a ten-minute self-indulgent whimper, I drive to our new home. Walking up the path to the door, the house just looks far too grown-up for us to live in. Just in time, David appears, grinning and with a huge bunch of flowers in his hand. He puts his arm around me and leads me carefully upstairs through the rubble, dust and bare plasterboard, past the loo – which has no door – and opens our bedroom door. It looks wonderful. Dave has dug out his grandpa's big red rug and unrolled it on the floor, our bed is all made up, there's a big lamp on in the corner and the chest of drawers is all polished, with the telly perched on top. He's a good and patient man. So what's he doing with me?

5 July
8 a.m.

Have a great night's sleep in the new house and am only semi-conscious when there's an almighty bang. Pulling myself up on to my elbows, I think there's been an explosion, but no. This bang, which I fear will become all too familiar over the coming weeks, heralds the arrival of the builders. They throw the front door open and storm in, whistling, shouting and clattering around the place. This is what life is to be like for the next wee while so I might as well get used to it.

6 July

In a celebratory mood. The loo now has a door! Simple things, eh? Although we must live on a building site for the time being, at least we have a toilet and a bed. Make a mature decision to rise above it all, keep working and breathe deeply. I mean, how bad can it get, for God's sake?

Week 22

16 July

Bad, bad, bad. From dawn till dusk our home is inhabited by lots of blokes whose bums hang out of their trousers. Sadly, mine also hangs out of my trousers now. Yes, it's true. I'm beginning to look like them – except I don't keep a copy of *The Daily Sport* under my oxter and whistle all the bloody time.

We all share the same loo, which is a bloody nightmare. In my present state I need to go *a lot* and so I loiter casually till they're out of eye and ear shot before tottering in to use it. They, on the other hand, take a minute or two to select their reading material – it's a hard call: *The Sun* or *The Sport*? – before stomping off with a jolly 'Just awa' for a s***e, pal. Back soon!', slamming the door and staying in there for hours. Hours! Not good for my blood pressure. Grrrrr.

18 July

This is a commune with no hippies in it. Every day as I lie in bed, the men march into the house first thing and shout, 'Morning, Alison, tea or coffee?' They're very sweet and mean well but I hate them all and wish they'd all bugger off. I want to be serene and relax when I'm not at work, not live in a sea of *Sun* newspapers, cups of sweet tea (milk 'n' two sugars) and builders' bums.

20 July

Fall out with the builders. I'm not sure if I just woke up grumpy. There they were, banging about and carrying on as usual and so I ask them to turn the bloody radio down.

'It's only on so we can listen to you, hen!' they lie, trying to soft-soap me.

'Well, turn the bloody thing off and you can listen to me now!' I suggest as I punch the off button. During the brief silence in which they try to compute what in God's name they've actually done – answer: nothing specific – I really push my luck and go on to say that, whilst they're at it, they can stop lying around the garden drinking lager and eating Kit Kats. At this they look quite shocked. I inhale deeply and explain that I'm hormonal and tired and that, much as I like them, I most definitely do not want their cheeky faces and out-of-proportion bottoms greeting the baby when we come home from the hospital in NOVEMBER, so to kindly get the finger out and finish the bloody house. With that I stomp out of the front door, slamming it behind me.

Week 23

21 July

No builders at all. God, and they say women are sensitive. LSH
has to go in as a peace envoy and whatever he says – perhaps
reinstating the Kit Kats and the lager on Fridays – does the
trick. Can't face the drilling, the whistling, the 'Cup of tea,
hen?' today, so Dave suggests I go and stay with my friend Fiona
for a few days. She lives in a flat in the West End, so at least I
can fool myself that I'm a groovy chick about town – as opposed
to a grumpy, pregnant woman surrounded by blokes whose
bums are hanging out of their trousers.

22 July

Being a flatmate again is great. Fiona and I go to the cinema,
eat hot dogs and Häagen Dazs ice cream with toffee sauce and
laugh our heads off! What would I do without my girlfriends?
I don't want to go home.

24 July

Despite myself, I've missed our soon-to-be house and return to
camp after work. It's quiet. I'm nervous. I enter the house. No
builders, no noise and no crap lying around the floor. I find
Dave looking worried.

  'Where are they? Have you killed them?' I ask.

  'No, I've told them to wait till we're on holiday and then they
can work their backsides off to have it finished by the time we
get home or they'll pay for us to live in a hotel.'

  'What a wonderful man you are,' I tell him, as I womble up
and give him a big smacker.

26 July
12 stone 9 pounds

Our holiday is imminent. We're off to Ireland by car for Mike and Mags' wedding and then to drive around and see the country. I've never been before and am really looking forward to it.

Now that I'm a ridiculous shape, though, I have to go and buy some clothes before we go anywhere. Every seam is stretching to splitting point.

After a rumble around the centre of Edinburgh, I'd like some sane human being over 10 stone in weight to tell me where in God's name you're supposed to get decent clothes? The choice seems to consist either of sacky, baggy black bags, dungarees or giant sailor suits. I do have one pair of jeans that have that strange stretchy waist thing, which are great – except they're brushed denim. Brushed denim! Do people think that the moment you become pregnant, all sartorial elegance is forgotten? Brushed denim and batik shirts. No wonder women hid for seven months in the '50s. Confinement wasn't about being confined in the house, it was about being confined in hideous clothes you wouldn't dream of being seen wearing out in public. Decide I'm going to be a maternity-wear designer.

Week 24

29 July

Still on the lookout for something to wear to the wedding. Despite the lack of choice, I have to buy a dress. Have huge protruding belly. Decide to buy big sizes rather than maternity sailor suit and plump (pun intended) for a dress from John Lewis's that is about a size 20. It hangs on me like an oversized bell-tent with me – the inflatable beanbag – stuffed inside. Not attractive. It suggests in a pregnancy magazine that you can compensate for your bump with a hat. In order to have a hat big enough to balance up my bump, I end up with something akin to a Mexican sombrero. Already thinking this when I put it on to show Dave – who promptly bursts out laughing, clicks his heels together and shouts, '*Andale! Andale!*' Prat.

31 July

Get the ferry to Ireland. It's the day before the wedding. We check into Kilkea Castle Hotel, which is gorgeous. Feel calm and in control and decide to run a bath. Enjoy a long soak, get out and scream. Dave rushes in to see what's happening. There's a hideous alien intruder, I shriek, gesticulating into the corner of the room. He gently points out it's just a full-length mirror. We don't have one at home and I never want to see one again. Ever. I can't believe that the Barbapapa look-alike is me! How can I go to my friends' wedding like that? People will think I'm the entertainment tent and open my dress looking for a Punch and Judy show. Slump into fat depression.

7 p.m.

Meet up with some old pals for dinner. I eat – they drink.

The ones I haven't seen for ages are amazed at my tummy. Some stroke it, others pat it but, whatever they do, they can't ignore it, that's for sure. I leave them in the bar speaking utter rubbish at midnight. Dave waddles me up to the bedroom.

'Don't spoil it for yourself,' I say, as he returns downstairs for more jollification.

As I lie in bed, windows wide open and feeling too damn hot, I reflect on the remark I've just made to him. 'Don't spoil it for yourself!' It seems I'm turning into my mother. What sort of '50s' claptrap is that? And all from the lips of the woman who, not eight months ago, fell asleep on the Christmas lunch table having 'spoilt it for herself' by going out the previous evening to a '70s' disco and dancing and drinking till the room wouldn't stop spinning and she couldn't remember the words to 'We Are Family' by Sister Sledge.

1 August

The wedding. Hot, sweaty and self-conscious – and that's just Dave after his previous night's intake. Looking around, it seems he's not alone. Everyone was plastered last night and, by the smell and the look of them, they're all at it again – and the wedding hasn't even started yet. I'll never drink again.

Lovely ceremony. Mags, who is Irish, looks wonderful in her gown and Mike looks so happy. There I sit sobbing in the church. Bloody hormones.

6.30 p.m.

All those who're not pregnant – i.e. everyone but me – is steaming again, dancing, laughing and whirling about. The Scots and the Irish together are a lethal combination. I say it once more, I'll never drink again.

7.30 p.m.

If you can't beat 'em, join 'em. Have two glasses of red wine and feel wonderful. Sit back and let everything wash over me.

10.30 p.m.

Alcohol should be banned. David's dancing around with my sombrero on his head. He's lent his sporran to some thin Irish girl, who's wearing it around her snake-like hips. I want to kill them both. Go to bed.

2 August

2 a.m.

Wake up. Can't sleep – too hot. Get up to open the window

32

and notice someone leaning against the doorway just opposite our room. I wave and am completely ignored. It seems that when you're pregnant, you're invisible – which is amazing given the size of me. Charming.

5 a.m.

David falls into bed and a drink-fuelled coma. His snoring is horrific. Want to hit him hard but can't get momentum up due to the bump. Pick up Dr M's book, briefly consider whacking Dave over the head with it to shut him up, but think better of it and decide to read it instead. Have a good look at the photograph of the woman who is seven months pregnant. I'm about four times the size and would rather wear a giant sailor suit on a date with George Clooney than have my photograph taken naked in my present state. Actually that goes for when I'm not pregnant as well. Let's be honest, there's no way she'd be getting her photograph taken if she had stretch marks, couldn't see her feet and all that fitted her was a giant sailor suit! Mark my words, even in pregnancy there's a conspiracy against normal-sized woman – well, normal-ish. Put the book down and stare at my gigantic tummy till sleep takes over.

Dream my tummy is made of cheese and Wallace and Gromit land on it in a space ship. When they realise it's just a gigantic tummy and not the moon, they pin their ears to it and listen to the baby's heart beat. Before I can find out what happens next, a huge snore wakes me up again. Give Dave the evil eye, but he's oblivious. Men.

8 a.m.

Might as well get up. King of the snorts is still asleep. Wander downstairs, only to see that the person I was waving at last night is in actual fact a suit of armour. So maybe I'm not as repellent as I thought. Cheer up slightly.

The car park and hotel is a scene of devastation. I'm the only person under sixty fit and well enough to eat breakfast. Sit with the mother and father of the groom and remember to avoid the mirror as I pack to leave while Dave lies in bed moaning.

3 August

Our last holiday before 'B'-day. We're driving around Ireland at the moment. It's the first time in ages we've spent any time together, so we start the discussions about babies' names. We stop at a petrol station and I buy an Irish baby name book. We start at the As and, by the time we get to the Bs, we agree we can't pronounce any of them. Go on to ones we know alphabetically. We can't agree on any at all. Keep stopping so I can stretch my bloated legs. Dave makes a complaint about my feet smelling.

'Swelling?' I ask.

'No, smelling,' he says. And this from a man who smells like a brewery. I naturally go into a huff and reluctantly take off the offending sandals. I can't believe it when he ties them together by their straps and hangs them off the tow bar of the car.

As we drive in silence there are lots of people peeping their horns and waving at us. God, this really is a friendly country, I say. It's not till we're in the streets of Waterford that a very kind bloke pulls up next to us at the traffic lights and says, 'Hey, did you know you've forgotten you've a pair of shoes hanging off the back of the car?' Just as David is about to say, 'It's my wife's feet, they're brutal,' I interrupt him with a 'Thank you very much indeed. I was wondering where they were,' before lumbering out of the passenger side and retrieving them. As soon as we're safely outside Waterford, we stop the car and put the shoes back outside – at which point all the horn-peeping and waving starts again. God, swelling and smelling. What a joy.

Week 25

4 August

David sees a loch and so stops the car and gets his fishing rod out. I stand by the side of it watching. All of a sudden I notice something is moving in the undergrowth beside me. Thinking that it may be a snake, I'm about to scream when the bracken parts and there lies the sorriest, most emaciated and sad-looking dog I've ever seen. I bend down and stroke it, the poor wee lamb, and, by the time David stops fishing, the dog and I are best friends. I'm not leaving him. LSH knows my hormones are making things 'difficult', so agrees to wrap up my bony new chum in a blanket and take him to the nearest police station to try and find the owners. We do so and the police say they don't recognise him but that maybe we should try the vet as he knows all the farms, dogs and so forth. So off we trundle to the local vet, who himself lives on a farm. He doesn't recognise the old soul either, but says he'll keep him in the barn overnight till he works out what to do. With a tear in the eye, we wave goodbye to the bony dog.

5 August

Wake up thinking about Bone Dog. I'm worried about him and can't get him out of my mind. At my insistence Dave takes me round to the vet after breakfast to check on his progress. We arrive and, as the vet's wife opens the door, she looks alarmed as she tells us, 'He's in the barn seeing to the dog.' For 'seeing to' read 'euthanasia'.

Realising immediately what is happening, Dave runs up to the barn door, bangs on it and shouts, 'Hello!'

The large wooden door slides open and the vet appears, complete with syringe.

'Is he . . . ?'

The vet shakes his head. 'No, you're just in time.'

'Right! We're taking the dog,' I declare dramatically.

So with a prognosis that is not good for old Bone Dog, we put him in the car and David – a.k.a. Saviour of the Mongrel, my hero – drives us to our next destination.

6 p.m.

David insists the dog sleeps in the car and not in the self-catering place we've rented. I burst into tears, which only underlines David's theory that my mothering instincts are coming out on the animal. I concede defeat as he's the Saviour of the Mongrel and wave to him – the dog, not Dave – as he's secured in the car till morning.

6 August
7 a.m.

Dave goes to let Bone Dog out of the car early, only to discover that both ends have exploded all over the place. The boot, the tartan rug, the back of the seats and – most dramatically – the golf clubs. This initially looks quite superficial but, as we find out much later, the contents of Bone Dog's bottom have even managed, rather impressively, to reach right down to the bottom of David's golf bag. It's the best laugh I've had in ages as Bone Dog lies watching a grown Scotsman shouting, stamping and swearing his head off. Not so funny now we have to travel in the car. Yuk.

Drive to our next destination with all the windows wide open. Absolutely bloody freezing, but know better than to complain. Now we're in Connemarra. First things first, though, we take Bone Dog straight to the local vet for a check-over and leave him there overnight.

7 August

The prognosis isn't good. Bone Dog may die, the vet says, he's terribly ill. He's in intensive care and we must wait to see what happens.

8 August

Bone Dog can't be moved. We extend our stay by a few days. We're very worried. David is also very stressed.

'The bloody restaurant isn't going to run itself!' he shrieks.

'You're a cruel and heartless capitalist,' is all I can muster as we fall into silence.

Week 26

13 August

Lying in bed in my hotel room reading Dr M. She warns against approaching ill animals or anything to do with dog or cat shit. You can even get a condition called toxoplasmosis. *Oh – my – God*. Read the symptoms. Develop all of them by the time Dave comes out of the bath. I declare I've got it and he'd better ship me to a hospital fast. LSH calms me down. He tells me to wait till morning 'cos I look OK and suggests I may have got myself into a lather about nothing. Brave man. I agree to wait.

14 August

7 a.m.

Wake Dave up.

'Phone the GP, please.'

9.01 a.m.

Dave has a long conversation with the doctor and comes off the phone telling me that our doctor, who's been practising for over twenty-five years, has never even *seen* a case of toxoplasmosis! And in any case, it's uncooked meats and *cat* shit you have to worry about.

'Are you sure he knows what the hell we're dealing with here?' I say.

'Yes,' says Dave, 'a women with an over-active imagination.' Braver than before, it seems. I suspect it's just 'cos he knows if I were to chase him I wouldn't stand a snowball's chance in Hell of catching him. I'm relieved that the baby and I are OK, so all we need to worry about now is our bony friend.

Week 27

19 August

Bone Dog lives! The vet, James – who is now our friend – has drip-fed and nurtured him and so he's now ready to come home. I'm delighted. David is neutral. I tell him he should be more like the vet and he suggests the vet wouldn't be quite so bloody nice if the dog had shat on *his* golf clubs, ruined *his* golf bag and left *him* completely skint thanks to an astronomical bill and all those extra days in the hotel waiting till the bloody dog was well enough to travel. Decide not to dwell on that.

20 August

As he's destined to live, Bone Dog has now been given the name Mullet, as David was fishing for red mullet when we found him. All three of us will live happily ever after in our home, awaiting the next new arrival in November.

21 August

Have been so preoccupied with Mullet that we virtually forget to rant and rave about the house. It's not till we're driving home on the last part of the journey that it all comes flooding back. Will the workmen be there? Will it be finished? Will we just keep on driving and not stop till we're back in Connemara and away from the dust, mess and buttocks?

We pull up outside the house and everything looks quiet. This could be good news – i.e. the job's complete and we have a home – or it could be bad: they knew we were away and have moved on to another job till they get death threats to tempt them back again.

'Wait here,' says Dave. He strides up to the front windows and peers in. My heart's in my mouth.

'Well?' is all I can manage and, when he turns back to me, he has a huge grin all over his face.

'They've done it!'

Done it! Yahoo! In fact, not only have they finished all the messy stuff but the carpets are down, the kitchen is in, the white goods are plumbed, the shower works and the loo is clean. I feel nothing short of euphoria. There is a god!

By the time we've unloaded the car – which takes much less time than it did to pack due to the lack of golfing equipment, rugs and small bags various – Bone Dog is pinned to the floor. He will not come out. I dig around in my bag and find a packet of biscuits I'd taken from the hotel room. I hold it under his nose. His eyes stare at it, he salivates but he's not going to move.

After ten minutes we give up and Dave reverses so that the boot, which we leave open, is right in front of the front door. We go in and unpack.

10 p.m.

Mullet is still in the car. Dave lifts him out, determined not to give him the opportunity to defecate in situ. So at least he's now on the grass outside, still pinned to the ground.

11 p.m.

Dave opens the shed door, gives Mullet a biscuit and retires for the night. We're exhausted and happy to be home.

22 August

Bone Dog emerges from the shed this morning, yawns and then sits by the back door. I open it up and invite him into the kitchen. He won't budge. He just sits, watching us. Fine. It's going to take time.

23 August

Back to work tomorrow. Feel much rested after our extended break. I've been so busy I haven't had a minute to think.

9.30 p.m.

Lying in bed, I think that the baby knows it's been at the back of my thoughts and starts kicking like a fiend. The feet are right under my rib cage and I can feel the heels. It's amazing and we sit and laugh at the active wee thing as it squirms around making its presence felt.

Decide on baby names. If it's a girl, it'll be Andi or Charlie and, if it's a boy, Louis or Keir.

Tell my friend in confidence, who points out that, 'They're all boys' names, you know.' I suppose they are. I feel in my waters that this baby is a boy. And I've plenty of water to feel it in, I can tell you.

Week 28

26 August

I'm in labour! I bloody am, I swear it! I rush off to phone the doctor, who asks me to explain exactly what's happening. After I calm down enough to describe what exactly *is* happening to me – i.e. I'm in labour – he says, 'It's Braxton Hicks.'

'An unusual name for a doctor,' I say.

'No,' he says, 'Braxton Hicks.'

'Oh, right. I think I had one of her albums in the '90s.'

'No, *Braxton Hicks*!'

These are sort of warm-up contractions, it seems. My tummy, which is big and tight and reminiscent of a drum anyway, suddenly tenses up like a huge clench and then releases again – a sensation known as Braxton Hicks. So, now I know that this is all normal – well, relatively speaking.

29 August

Mullet's still spending his nights in the shed, but now spends most of his days sitting at the back door, staring in with his nose pressed up against the glass. I leave the door open with a trail of biscuits leading in, trying to tempt him to cross the threshold, but so far to no avail. Och, in his own good time.

30 August

Even in the time I've been away, I'm finding it more difficult to reach all the CD players and record decks in the studio, so kind and lovely Boss opts to have the engineers cut a chunk of wood out of the front to accommodate my bump. He's not such a monster after all.

31 August
13 stone 2 pounds

Weigh myself – bad move. Good God, I know I ate the odd bit of Irish bread, but I seem to be expanding by the moment! According to my manual, the baby's currently laying down stores of fat and iron. Like baby, like mother, I think. Its skin's also becoming a lot paler and less wrinkled. Mmmm, that's where the resemblance ends then.

Week 29

3 September

Hormones are hell. Walking along Princes Street, I see a man begging in a doorway and I burst into tears. For God's sake, I must get a grip on myself. The bloke was wearing Calvin Klein jeans, smoking fags and talking on his mobile. I mean, he didn't look too hard done by to me. In fact, I think I may have detected a look of sympathy in his eye when he saw me – a giant sailor-suited balloon shuffling along, out of breath.

4 September
8.30 a.m.

Do the usual trick with Mullet, open the door and lay out the trail of biscuits before going upstairs for a shower.

8.50 a.m.

Back in the kitchen after I've dressed, I go to put the kettle on and suddenly feel an ice-cold thing on my leg. Aaargh! I almost hit the roof – which is quite impressive, given my current shape and weight.

Twirling round, I spot Mullet scrabbling to get under the kitchen table. It must have been his magnificent Irish nose pressing against my leg and alerting me to his arrival inside. Poor old thing got more of a shock than I did.

9.10 a.m.
Still under the table with Mullet, trying to cajole him out of his shivering.

11.30 a.m.
Buy a blanket from the charity shop for £1 and introduce him to it as his new bed under the kitchen table. He seems rather pleased. I think he realises that he's here to stay.

Week 30

9 September
David's sister Kirsty and her husband are going out and ask us to baby-sit. We're very excited at the prospect. Wee Amy is three months old and we're very keen to play at being parents.

When we arrive, she has just had a bottle and is settled down to sleep. Kirsty and Al leave. Dave and I sit and watch TV, taking turns to walk through and see the wee one sleeping.

10 p.m.
Amy wakes up and we both run to the cot and look bemused.

'I'll do it,' I say gamely, settling myself down in a chair with a bottle. It's a wonderful feeling, sitting there with the wee baby in my arms while she drinks her bottle. I can't believe that in just a few weeks we'll have one of our own.

12 September
First National Childbirth Trust class. Meet Dave in the car park of the local school where they're held. We enter the room.

A large blowsy hippy introduces herself and then goes round the room asking the four assembled couples to do the same. Three of the men are called David and three of the women are called Alison. Can't believe it. I start giggling, catch Dave's eye and he starts giggling too. We face away from each other, but I can feel his shoulders going up and down – so are mine. I retire to the loo to laugh. I think I've got it out of my system when I come back into the room and see Dave. I'm off again. There's nothing that can be done – we've lost it.

After another ten minutes of deeply disapproving looks from the woman running the class, I just want to go. Beanbags – pushing – placenta: it doesn't matter what she says, it seems absolutely hysterical.

At last she suggests a break and offers everyone a tea or coffee. They all order 'decaf', but I think, 'Bugger that, I'm not giving up coffee as well.' I swig back my fully caffeinated brew.

13 September
3 a.m.

Well, I certainly learned several things tonight.

1. The NCT do not condone the use of drugs. They think breathing and gas and air should see you through. I'm not sure about this. I'll do a straw poll amongst friends.

2. There are a lot more Davids and Alisons in Edinburgh than I ever previously imagined. Are Davids inexplicably attracted to Alisons? Do Alisons find Davids utterly alluring? Is it nothing to do with physical attraction and all in the moniker our parents choose for us?

3. The only reason I'm considering all this rubbish is because I'm lying awake, head like a toyshop. So maybe – just maybe – the decaf coffee thing has some merit after all. Great, so now my tolerance to the one final

stimulant I was permitted to indulge in has left the
building. Shite.

Lie awake for hours reliving over and over again our prepubescent performance at the NCT class. I'm now convinced
we're far too irresponsible to be parents. The poor child within
my expanding bump doesn't know what he/she's in for. Poor
wee thing.

15 September

Go to a friend's leaving do at work. Starts reasonably enough in
a bar. Everyone fagging away. One thing I haven't fancied at all
is smoking.

As the night progresses, the singing and dancing starts and
everyone has had a load to drink. I've had a glass of red wine.
I don't even like red wine, but hey – it's better than bloody
nothing.

11 p.m.

I'm really getting into the swing of things now. The singing
starts up again, I get carried away with the whole thing and I
have a fag. I smoke a cigarette. Yes, I do. I take a long white
stick from a packet, put it to my lips and light it. Not only do
I light it, I then proceed to inhale it – to my boots. I feel light-
headed and sick. I think I might pass out. The taste is revolting.
I'm revolting. I'm an irresponsible, revolting mother-to-be.

Get a taxi home.

Week 31

16 September

Wake up racked with guilt What the hell did I do that for?
How could I smoke? I haven't even given the damn weed a

second thought since March and there I was, puffing away like Fag Ash Lil last night. Have palpitations. I tell Dave, who tells me to calm down, everything will be fine.

I rush to get my manual. Yes, it's true. I must have starved my baby of oxygen during the inhalation process. I'm disgusted with myself. If anything is wrong with this child, it'll be all my fault. I hate myself. I stay in bed. I call work. I can't face it. I'm not worthy of a womb.

3 p.m.

LSH tells me to stop being so dramatic and then goes on to list several women – all of whom shall remain nameless – who smoked their heads off during their entire pregnancies and went on to give birth to perfectly healthy babies. He tells me I'm being irrational and that one cigarette does not a defect make. Feel a bit better, which he knows only too well when I ask, 'Have you got any Silk Cut?' Just joking!

19 September

My birthday. Wake up to find a huge present wrapped up by our bed. Open it up only to discover a long sausage-shaped cushion designed for placing between my knees so as to balance up my bump and help me get some sleep. Try to whip up a big, genuine, thank-you grin, but can't help wishing it was a tissue-paper-wrapped selection of lingerie from Janet Reger or a 40-foot bar of chocolate.

Supposed to go back to the NCT class tonight. Can't face it. It's my birthday – I don't want to roll around on beanbags with every David and Alison in the East of Scotland. We skive, keeping our prepubescent behaviour up to scratch.

Week 32

23 September

Dr M says I should be exercising regularly. Oops.

So far I've managed to avoid all exercise, bar taking Mullet to the park for a waddle. Reading about labour, though, I realise I must get fitter, so decide to walk to work. It's about 4 miles from the house and by the time I arrive it has taken me hours. According to Maureen, the receptionist, my face is bright red and I look like I may combust. Am given the day off work and a taxi home. So it seems exercise is bad for me – a suspicion I've held for years.

25 September

Finish radio programme and am told that Boss wants to see me. Lumber upstairs to the third floor and settle into a large chair. He appears with a stern face.

'Remember the traffic warden?'

I nod. How could I forget?

'Well,' he says in his most grim voice and with his scary eyes darting around, 'the complaint about you has been upheld by the Radio Authority.'

As I feel the tears welling up I ask, 'Are you going to sack me?'

'Sack you? *Sack* you? Good God, no!' he shouts enthusiastically, opening a bottle of champagne. 'This is *fantastic*! Well done! We couldn't buy this bloody publicity!' And then he proceeds to show me the coverage in the newspapers, both national and local, before handing me a list of interviews that the papers are wanting to do with me.

At this point the Head of News interjects to ask me if I will dress up as a traffic warden for a photo opportunity. I point out that getting a bell-tent-sized uniform might prove tricky. He says he can get one. I tell him to bugger off. Watch as Boss and Head of News get trollied. Och well, at least they're happy and I've still got a job.

26 September

NCT class tonight. We meet in the car park. Dave is fraught from work and I'm very tired, so we decide to skive off and go for a curry instead.

9 p.m.

Fluttering is more of a jamming of limb against stomach wall these days. Not only can Dave feel it, but he can also see it as an angry little foot comes whopping out from the skin on my belly. It looks very *Alien* – just before the thing leaps out of John Hurt's stomach.

27 September

Dave has a pal who sells prams. We know we must address the equipment side of life soon, so we arrange to drive over and go pram-hunting.

We arrive in the shop and are amazed at the array of para-phernalia available for children. Eek. We need a *Rough Guide to Baby Stuff* but, as no one has written one, we have to go with our instincts. We attach ourselves to the salesman and let him guide us. And guide us he does.

All prams are blue. Why? They're all blue and puffy and not in the least bit groovy. There are big coachy prams and amazingly-easy-to-change-into-at-least-five-different-things prams. We go for the latter – yes, it is more expensive but it's a pram-cot-buggy in one.

You'll need a changing-bag, we're told. Not wanting to seem

stupid, we say, 'Of course, yes, we'll have one to match the pram.'

Soon we're being talked into a Moses basket.

'The pram can be used as a cot, can't it?'

'Yes, but the Moses basket is a traditional crib for the newly born little baby.'

Sold to the woman with the rampaging hormones.

'What's that chest of drawers for?'

'Oh, that's a changing table.'

'What're they for?'

'Well, the baby lies on top here and the edges stop the little angel from rolling off and hurting his delicate little self.'

Sold – to the same woman, now not only with the rampaging hormones but the effortlessly lighter wallet.

Next, a cot. Well, as far as I can make out we've already got two – the cot that is part of the pram and the Moses basket.

'Ah yes, but they don't stay that small for long,' he said, guiding us through to the mahogany, four-poster Queen Anne Cot Department. My parents had said they would buy us a cot, so we select one that has so many safety guarantees and is so substantial that, when we're finished with it, it'll be dug into the ground outside our house and used as a bunker in case of a nuclear winter. Sold to the woman with the light wallet, the big tummy and the worried face. How are we going to fit all this stuff into our house?

We leave with a nappy incinerator, a bill that brings us out in a rash and a bemused look in our eyes. We had no idea. None. It's a different world. All the stuff, the terminology, the money! Jeez.

Week 33

30 September

Against all odds, I take back my initial doubts about the sausage cushion. It works. It's also handy for jabbing David on the head or back with when his snoring gets out of hand. A good present after all.

3 October

Weigh myself – 14 stone. No, this is not a misprint – *14 bloody stone*. Want to live alone in a cave.

4 October
14 stone 1 pound

Oh – my – God! At this rate I'll combust before birth. At a pound a day I'll weigh about 16 stone by the time I give birth. Seek solace in the fridge.

5 October

Meet friend Gordon for lunch. He can't stop staring at my tummy. I haven't seen him since before I got pregnant. He can't believe it. Everyone in the restaurant thinks he's the father and keeps smiling and asking him if he's looking forward to it.

'Oh, it's not mine,' he admits jauntily, leaving all the women looking at him with big cow eyes and thinking, 'Oh, imagine taking her *and* a baby on and when she's *that* fat! What a lovely guy.'

Gordon suggests that he's inadvertently stumbled on the perfect way to pick up women. I agree and then suggest that their attitude may change slightly when this martyr man suddenly starts trying to get off with them. Back to the drawing board.

Week 34

6 October

Have an overwhelming urge for anchovies. I hate anchovies, but I can't think about anything else in the world. Fully believe I'll kill someone if I don't get anchovies into my throat now! Can't stop myself from talking about it on my radio programme either. Ten minutes later a huge pizza – completely covered in anchovies – arrives from the local pizzeria. I love them truly, madly, deeply. Wolf down the lot in between tracks and then have a jar of the little suckers in salty oil as a chaser. Gads, I love them. Help me, I'm mutating into an anchovy-eating alien.

7 October
14 stone 3 pounds

Hells bells, I'm inflating in front of my very eyes! I may have to weigh my swollen feet down with lead boots in case I float away.

9 October

Last day at work. Arrive feeling quite emotional, only to be told that I smell of fish. Remind them about the anchovies, but then feel so paranoid I go to the local chemist and buy a toothbrush and toothpaste. Bloody anchovies.

Boss comes down to say goodbye to me on air. Can't believe I actually start crying – on air, on my radio show! They'll think my entire personality has been a ruse. The bolshie, cheeky woman I was seems to have disappeared – replaced by some apron-wearing housewife from the '50s. I'll be swapping recipes soon, I know it.

11 October

Pelvic floor exercises. Came up today whilst in for a check-up. Great. I'd forgotten them! Am given the sad, patronising eye of the midwife, who all but tut-tuts at me whilst shaking her head. What a bad, evil and silly girl, her expression says. So, as we sit here, I clench my undercarriage at her in much the same way as I used to stick my tongue out behind a teacher's back at school after getting told off. Take that!

12 October

This day will go down in history as the day in which my last semblance of independence is taken from me. Sob. David wrestles the car keys off me. Admittedly I've taken to crashing a lot recently – but only because I can't turn round and so just reverse till I hit the car behind me. That's what bumpers are for, I object, but he ignores me completely, whips the keys out of my hand and – I may add – continues with his normal life! Take comfort in a couple of jars of anchovies. They do perk a person up.

Week 35

14 October

What time of year is Lent? I've got a real beauty for when it comes along – giving up sleeping! Maybe I can do it in lieu of actual Lent, because I've completely given up sleeping now. There's no position at all that's comfortable to lie in. On my back I panic, as my tummy is so huge I may suffocate myself.

On my side with the sausage-shaped pillow between my knees I can get a little rest. If I'd had the bloody pillow between my knees that night in February, I wouldn't be in this predicament in the first place. Realistically, though, dozing is the best I can manage – dozing whilst being kicked and squirmed internally and aurally traumatised by David's snoring externally. Have decided to invent some sort of suspended animation chamber for pregnant women to sleep in – a sort of vertical floatarium where you have no weight on you or the baby and you can just bobble round with your head poking out the top sleeping soundly. Speaking of water, excuse me, I must go – again . . .

16 October

It's one week since I stopped work and I'm now going mad – mad – *mad* with boredom. Most of the day is spent waddling to the loo and back. At least that's the exercise angle taken care of. Must be covering miles of carpet every day. Grrrrr . . . I'm going back to work the minute this baby is born. It's not going to change *my* life, that's for sure.

18 October

Doctor's appointment. The baby's engaged. Congratulations! Apparently this means the head is down and it's getting ready for action. Very exciting.

Week 36

20 October

Buy a video camera. We agreed we should have one of our own now to record the joys of parenthood and the first moments of our little baby.

Read the instructions and work it all out. Dave has an aversion to all things technical and I know he's largely ignoring me as I give him a crash course when he comes in with one eye on *The Scotsman* and the other eye on the clock as he's going out to some dinner or other. Oh well, I guess I'll be taking on the Speilberg duties in this family.

21 October
2 a.m.

Speilberg starts earlier than planned. Father-to-be went out at eight last night and has just come back. Not only do I know this 'cos I'm up every two hours peeing anyway, but he forgot his keys so I have the added bonus of waking up to the doorbell going, the dog barking and panic setting in. *Oh – my – God!* Who *is* that at the door in the middle of the night?

A quick look under the bedclothes proves that it's the sausage cushion not Dave that's making the humpy back in the bed. I lumber downstairs and open the door, as the man formerly known as David falls in. He's trying to be all affectionate whilst breathing fumes from Hell over my face. God. He soon falls into a deep, wheezy sleep on the sofa and as I lie upstairs unable to get back to sleep, I have a brain-wave. Taking the camera out of its new box, I go down to film the snoring monster. I film him for about three minutes – the decibel level impressively high and the strange fluid drooling out of his mouth fairly substantial. Lovely.

8.30 a.m.

Up and downstairs. As I eat my Weetabix, I hear groaning coming from the lounge. I shuffle through to see the pathetic sight of a grown man – his body looking dislocated – still in full Highland dress, lying on the couch with his hands over his eyes. I wish him a good morning and offer him a cup of tea. I'm surprised he doesn't smell a rat at this stage. Previous experience of the aftermath of coming home in that less than fragrant state would have suggested he'd have got the evil eye for at least half a day. Add to that the hormones that are coursing through my body and I'm genuinely surprised he isn't locked in the toilet cowering. But the half-asleep doughball just mumbles 'Yes' and happily accepts a mug of hot, sweet tea.

As he props himself up on one elbow, I saunter to the TV and turn it on 'for the news'. And, before he can object, there he is – taking up all 26 inches of our Panasonic surround-sound TV screen. He looks confused as he focuses on the great, open-mouthed, roaring beast, ruddy-faced with spittle bubbling out of its mouth.

'What the f***?' is all he manages to utter before it dawns on him he's watching his alter ego – 'Pish-head Man'. I swear I think I'm going to give birth laughing.

23 October

Chat about pelvic floors again today with some mates. The topic and pace of conversation has changed completely for me. Gone is the need to discuss Nicole Kidman's latest fashionable offering. No, no, no, it's all to do with breasts, vaginas and cervices. Nice. The uterus is today's discussion point and what the plural is. 'Uterus-es'? 'Uteri'? 'Uterum'?

24 October
Birth Plan

Keep pants on till last moment.
Bob Marley during first stages of labour.
John Martyn for actual birth and immediate aftermath.
Pain relief as requested.
No Dustbuster (a.k.a. Ventouse).

Low lights during birth so as not to give baby a shock.
Bacardi and Coke and a mobile phone immediately afterwards

25 October

I've begun to look longingly at joggers. Do they know how lucky they are being able to run? Do they? Being able to move their legs so close to each other in a back-and-forth action whilst moving quickly? Lucky bastards. I'll take up jogging after the baby's born. It's a wonderful expression of the human body. Meanwhile, I can't even see my blasted feet. LSH has to tie my laces. I feel like a giant, incontinent child prone to outbursts of sobbing.

Week 37

30 October

Friend Jeffy comes round. She's one of my few friends who has a baby. She hands me a parcel. How sweet, I think, until I realise it's a large, waterproof mattress cover.

'What in God's name is that for?'

'It's in case your waters break whilst you're in bed.' Lovely.

'Will Dave ever love me again – waterpoof mattresses, a stomach like a barrage balloon, over four stone more than I weighed just a few months ago?' I ask.

'Well,' she replies, 'at least you haven't got piles!' True.

1 November

Guess what? I've got piles. The only part of me that seemed to be retaining some sort of normality has now gone. I can't even reach to apply the stuff you're supposed to apply to the damn things. Unbelievably sore. Not amused. It's official: piles are pants.

Week 38

2 November

Two weeks till my due date. Am on a jar of anchovies a day and drinking gallons of raspberry leaf tea, which is supposed to make the labour faster. Sadly, neither of the aforementioned have made a blind bit of difference to the haemorrhoids, though someone did share the tip that Preparation H is excellent for the face. As my face now looks like a bloated arse, it seems only right in some strange way.

The practicalities of what is just around the corner are starting to dawn on me now. I've no idea what to do or to expect. Get Dr M out again and have a browse. Bloody hell! Don't fancy it one little bit.

3 November
3 a.m.

Can't get the Dr M stuff out of my head. How's that baby going to come out of there? It just doesn't make sense, does it? I'm not some kind of snake whose jaws unhook. I think I want pain relief now.

4 November

Hospital tour today. Choose to go to one on the far side of the city because people say it has a cottagey feel. On the way we get stuck in a traffic jam and, as I sit there gazing out the window, my eyes fix on a billboard with a picture of a white sandy beach, turquoise sea and a girl lying on a lounger drinking a large glass of Bacardi and Coke. Oh, yes please. By the time I've given my instructions to David – 'The first thing I want after the baby is born is a large Bacardi and Coke' – we're there.

Cottagey? I'd say more ancient and run-down myself. However, today we'll be taken around the labour ward to familiarise ourselves with the equipment. The very word 'equipment' brings me out in lumps – or at least it would if I had room left for any more!

We're met at reception by an efficient-looking woman who guides us through to a waiting-room where another four or five couples stand looking equally overawed and lost. She soon starts the tour. As she goes through it all, she lists the equipment, produces things and waves them around. If this is supposed to put your mind at rest, I'm a monkey's uncle. There's a thing called a ventouse that looks like a Dustbuster and – coincidentally – performs a similar function. It literally sucks the baby out if it doesn't make its own way in good time. We see needles, giant forceps, monitors, tubes and gels. I just want to be given a general anaesthetic now and have them bring me round in about a month.

5 November

Friend asks me what school the baby's going to. Is she serious? Is she bloody *serious*? I've more pressing issues on my mind – like, oh! that's right, I can't see my feet, I've piles the size of Inverness hanging out of my backside and, excuse me for bringing it up, but there's still the small matter of giving birth. Bugger education and the horse it rode in on, I tell her. She leaves quite shortly after that. Perhaps I was a little blunt.

6 November

Meet friends for a decaf. A good chat but no caffeine high, so I go retail strolling instead. Can't buy anything – I just gaze into shop windows dreaming of the day I'll be able to wear a nice pair of Levis 501s and ditch brushed-denim forever.

I'm in one shop stroking size 12 clothes lovingly when the shop assistant asks me if I'm pregnant?

'No, actually I'm just fat,' I snap back. Well, what a stupid question.

Dave's amused at this story, but soon realises I don't share his sense of hilarity when I throw a pint of water over him. Yes, I think, we're in agreement. I'm ready to have this baby as the mood is not improving.

7 November

Dave wrestles the waterproof mattress cover on to the bed and we practise putting nappies on my teddy. I think we're really getting the hang of it. Have packed my case for hospital because it could literally be any day now. Have a nightie, dressing-gown, book, make-up bag, lots of Bob Marley CDs and, of course, baby clothes. Dr M says we'll need three vests, three sleep-suits and some socks. They're all in.

Can't believe the cot that Dave has just built is going to have a real live baby in it in a few days. I just can't believe it. The wee room next to ours is ready for lift-off. The ceiling has blue-sky wallpaper on it and the walls have Walt Disney characters on a background of yellow. So, boy or girl, it'll be fine.

Very pleased. I think the nappy-changing technique could be worse. And I think we're ready. I do. We are.

Week 39

12 November
1 p.m.

Out for an Italian lunch with my chum Fiona. Sit for hours eating pasta and gossiping. When I decide to go home, I ask the waiter to phone me a taxi.

Within seconds, some bloke rushes over and says, 'I'll take you! I'll take you!'

'Where exactly are you going to take me?' I asked.

'To hospital!' he shouts indignantly. I'm now so huge people assume I'm in labour at all times. We have a good laugh when I explain I'm just going home and am not allowed to drive anymore 'cos I keep crashing the car.

13 November
1 a.m.

Was that psychic? Wake up with a sore stomach. Excessive laughter, spicy pasta and a drive over the cobbles in an Edinburgh taxi may have done the trick. Four days to go and unable to see my feet for the last five weeks, so I hope to God it has. Look at LSH, who's lying sleeping sweetly. Bastard. I haven't slept in eight weeks. If I'm not shuffling to the loo every ten minutes due to the baby lying on my bladder, then I'm being used as target practice internally.

6 a.m.

Stomach much sorer. *Oh – my – God*, this is it! Early! It can't take after me then.

Wake LSH up with the help of the sausage cushion. He looks grumpy till I tell him I think the baby's coming, and he's up and out of his bed like a ferret up a drainpipe. It's remarkable. He runs around the house about seventeen times trying to look useful but not managing in the least. Eventually I sit him down, make him a cup of tea and tell him to breathe deeply. Bloody hell!

8 a.m.

Am floating in a large bath. We wait till the water goes cold, then top it up. After an hour in there all my toes and fingers are wrinkled up and I decide it's doing no good whatsoever so get out. Ouch! Get back in again as quickly as a beached whale can. It seems the water is, in actual fact, doing a hell of a lot of good.

10 a.m.

The pain is getting unbearable. I get out of the bath and slap on the Tens machine. Over the years I've tried every slimming technique known to woman – even been wrapped up in mud, cling film and bandages. But call it what you like, the Tens machine is a Slendertone machine. It is. There are straps you attach to your back and the electric current pulses through to counteract the contractions. That's Slendertone and I should know, having spent hours strapped to the thing in the late '70s – all to no avail, I reminisce. Ouch! Much like this. We manage to pretend to watch an Open University programme on the atom and then I put on my Bob Marley CD to calm me, LSH and the baby down. It doesn't work at any level, so we bite the bullet and decide it's time to go to hospital.

11 a.m.

Shown into a reception room where a midwife comes in and asks me a few questions. I hand over my birth plan and – if I'm not mistaken – get a fairly wry smirk from the recipient.

'Thanks,' she says and doesn't even glance at it. She then has a look at me and tells me I'm 4 cm dilated.

'Is that good?' I ask optimistically.

'Yes,' she said, but I don't believe her. As far as I can remember, Dr M says you have to be 10 cm dilated to really get the show on the road. Oh well, at least I'm now in pain-relief alley. I'm asked if I want to walk around. No, I don't or I would've walked around at home. I keep my polite face on, though, and tell her it's actually quite sore. She gets me some gas and air. Mmmm, I like this.

12 p.m.

Shit-a-doodle-dandy, this is sore! These great contractions are very regular now. Dave goes off to find a midwife, who comes in and examines me again.

In hospital lying on a bed with three men staring up my dressing-gown. I tell them I intend to keep my pants on till the last possible minute. They look at each other, whip them off and proceed to discuss my nether regions like I'm not there at all. I wish I wasn't.

It seems I'm still only 4 cm dilated. How can that be? What's been going on with bloody contractions then? The midwife shrugs and asks me if we'd like to get things going?

'How do "we" do that?' I ask.

'We can break your waters,' she says. 'That should help.'

Seems reasonable, I think, and so I say OK. Of course, I have no idea – no idea at all. Yes. No. Oh, I don't know. I'm thirty-one years old and I haven't got a clue. Not a Scooby Doo. Just say, 'Yes.'

Next thing I know, another midwife appears with a thing that looks like a mammoth crochet hook. Oh, that's nice, she's going to do some knitting and chat while I labour, I naively think. If only. The truth is that this instrument of torture is headed up my front bottom and into my nether regions where she presumably knits one and purls one before my water does, in point of fact, break. Stand back – man the lifeboats – we're off, I think.

1 p.m.

So here we are an hour later and, as a matter of fact, we aren't 'off' at all. The next thing my little S&M friend comes up with is a drip.

'A drip? What the hell's that for?'

'Oh, speeds things up,' she says. I've heard that somewhere before. So anyway, off we go again. This now means I'm stuck flat on my back on the bed with an intravenous drip in my arm. In the stuff goes and there we sit – Dave reading the Sunday papers and me listening to John Martyn on the CD. It's about now I decide I'm coming back as a man in my next life.

1.45 p.m.

Things have really started happening. Great waves of giant period pains come every four minutes . . . every three minutes . . . until they're every minute. Get stuck into the gas and air, which is quite good actually. Makes me laugh which, given the circumstances, is a surprise, I can tell you. I decide I'll go into the gas and air business. Really, what a great way to get my legs waxed or – even more appropriately – my bikini-line done. Suggest this to midwife, who ignores me.

Shortly after this the really, *really* bad pains seem like a gentle tickle. There are some big mothers coming my way now and there are no swear words strong enough to describe them so when I screech, 'Get me some drugs!' Dave knows I mean it.

Ten minutes later I get a shot of diamorphine. I ask for half a shot 'cos I don't want to be too out of the game. Mmmm – I like this. Everything slows down and looks like I'm watching through jelly specs. I feel calm and floaty and smile. Must have been good drugs.

In good time this wears off too.

'What next?' I ask my narcotics provider.

'Gas and air?' she asks.

Gas and air? Completely useless! 'Bring on the epidural!' I scream.

The anaesthetist comes in. Dave knows him and they have a little chat. He was in the restaurant last night for dinner. Do I care? Do I f***! Get your needle out and get the pain relief going, boys, this isn't some cocktail party, you know!

Obviously I don't say this, I just lie there wishing to God someone would press a fast-forward button and I'm at home,

Doris Day-like, in a gingham frock with a perfect, pink, powdered baby in a large pram in the garden as I bake scones. Can gas and air make you hallucinate?

Epidural doesn't work. It doesn't work! I can't remember Dr M warning me about that. I can still feel everything and – *Oh – my – God!* . . . you have no idea how much I wish I couldn't. Gulp gas and air as if there's no tomorrow.

Start composing a letter to Dr M in between contractions. Highlight what seem to me like several omissions, including the chapter about crouching on all fours, bellowing like a bison and biting your husband's hand.

11 p.m.

Midwife tells me the baby will be born in two hours.

Three minutes later she shouts, 'Push!'

'No way!' I shout back. 'I don't want to have a crap in front of my husband,' and point-blank refuse.

'Push!' she shouts again, 'Push!'

Eventually I can resist no more and so the baby arrives in the world like a bullet. She gamely catches it and then we clock him – small, pink, squinting up at us as we squint down at him. It's a he. Him. All 6lb 13 oz of him. Small, sweet and, within fifteen seconds, pulling at my right breast. Good God! I'm not sure about this at all.

11.30 p.m.

Midwife takes the baby and hands him to David, announcing she's going to 'stitch me up'.

At this point she turns a lamp similar to the ones the Nazis must have used for interrogation right on to my nether regions and sets to work. I wonder if she remembers I've had no anaesthetic in the area. Apparently not, I realise, as she jabs her needle into me. I leap away screaming and she looks up from her place of work with an angry grimace.

'I can't work with you if you're going to be like that!' she shouts. She does, she shouts. I'm perhaps in the most vulnerable position I've ever been in in my life, I don't know what's going on, David doesn't know what's going on and all I want to be is Doris Day, with a newborn baby in a bed with white sheets tucked in around me, wearing a lemon-coloured cotton nightie and being kissed on the forehead by the proud father as we sit serenely looking forward to the future. But by the bad luck of the draw, I now have this bully of a woman holding me down. I remind her, in a very calm voice, that the epidural hasn't worked and that I can feel everything.

'Oh,' she says and wanders off. Now, had I been the normal me I'd have leapt up, got her by the scruff of the neck and held her against a wall whilst demanding she tell me why such a God-awful butcher as herself went into a so-called caring profession when she clearly couldn't give a toss. But I don't. I'm in shock.

14 November
12.05 a.m.

Midwife comes back with a friend, who watches as she tries it all again. Eventually I muster up enough gumption to say, 'I want to see a consultant *now*!' Rolling her eyes, she leaves and eventually returns with a doctor, who gives me a local anaesthetic and finishes the job.

12.30 a.m.

Exhausted but can't sleep. Want to sleep – can't sleep, the undercarriage is still being stitched up. It'll look like a road map down there once they've finished – if they ever finish.

1.15 a.m.

Back in my bed at last – in a ward full of other shocked-looking women. Our small baby is asleep in the cot, whilst I just lie there shaking and throbbing in all the wrong places. I think I'm in real shock. This is not shivering but shaking. There's no one to ask if this is normal. What the hell *is* 'normal'? This isn't, I'm sure of that. Drop off eventually.

4 a.m.

Wake up and just lie there looking into the cot. I can't believe that the little person wrapped up in a blanket and sound asleep is mine. Is ours. Is the little life I've had in my body for the past nine months. It just doesn't seem real. I can't really move much other than to look round to see Dave – who has managed to doze off – and then lie back down again. I feel like I've been run over.

7 a.m.

Nudged awake with the help of a midwife.

'The baby needs feeding,' she declares.

As she wrestles the baby from his sleeping position in the cot, I wrestle my right mammary out for another shot. There is general disinterest on both sides. After ten minutes we give up. I close my eyes.

9 a.m.

Awake again. This time it's a brave woman wanting to ask me a few questions. She begins to talk to me about contraception. I can't believe what I'm hearing. I tell her there's no point – I'm never having sex again as long as I live, so she may as well leave now and fast, before I hit her with a bedpan.

10 a.m.

Mum and Dad arrive for a look at their new grandson – wee Louis Alexander Mackie Scott.

'He looks like Yasser Arafat,' Dad declares as I gaze adoringly at my little bundle. Ignore Dad as Mum oohs and aahs over him. LSH arrives with two bags full of Marks & Spencer's food. The hospital food is bowf, he declares as he digs out a prawn cocktail and a chicken tikka sandwich. I eat them hungrily until I realise that what goes in must come out. Sooner or later I'll have to go to the toilet. *Oh – my – God!* The thought of any movement on that front frankly puts the fear of God in me. Check the M&S bag for a bottle of rum. There isn't one. It seems I'll have to take this hideous task on in a state of sobriety.

12 p.m.

Nature calls. It takes me thirty seconds to get into a vertical position. Are my innards going to fall out? I swing my legs over the side of the bed and think I'm going to pass out. Shakily, I get to my feet and shuffle a bit till I get my dressing-gown on. I feel like an 110-year-old woman. Moving in any way whatsoever has taken on a new dimension of horror altogether. The traditional one-leg-in-front-of-another routine is something I haven't had to think about for thirty-odd years and now, after passing the equivalent of a bowling ball through my front bottom, it's frankly agony.

Get to the cubicle and steel myself for the inevitable. I'm scared and feel like all my insides are coming out. Half-expect to wake up in theatre – not singing and dancing on stage, but being operated on by a surgeon putting them all back in again. Survive the experience and, as I shuffle back, I swear that if I ever see the midwife again, I'll kill her.

Every ten minutes there's someone coming in to talk at me. I can't really listen – I just want to stare at the wee pink baby in the cot next to me and marvel at the fact that he's our son. The wee darling. I'm handed samples of baby cream and nappies, asked to fill in a questionnaire and shown how to bathe and change him. It's too much to take in. There's constant noise and it's so hot. At least my shaking has stopped. But I'm a mess and I wish they'd all just go away. Dave tells the nurses not to let any more visitors in.

I'm warned that after three days I might get a little weepy. Bullshit! I'm a mature, level-headed woman. Clearly I'll not be indulging in that old nonsense in three days. I think I'll just start now.

16: November
10.30 a.m.

I detect a slight size change in the chest area. I was warned this would happen. It's apparently my milk coming in and thus I finally bite the bullet and dispatch a confused-looking David to purchase a maternity bra from Mothercare.

11.45 a.m.

Bless him, he's back and with the biggest one he can find. As I flip open the box, I pull it – in all its gigantic glory – out. It can easily accommodate two particularly voluptuous traffic cones!

'Christ, you could put a couple of watermelons in here and still have room for *my* boobs!' I laugh, warning him to get the engine running because he'll be going right back to exchange it for something altogether more human-sized. I pad through to the bathroom to try it on and demonstrate my hilarious joke.

Sob. It doesn't even get halfway there. It's like a G-string. It's useless! I briefly toy with the idea of an making an SOS call to a local scaffolding company, but can't bear the thought of a quantity surveyor having to measure me up. Looking on the bright side, at least I won't have to meet him – I mean, I can just hoist my pendulous gino-breasts out the window up here and down to him!

3 p.m.

I've got to get out of this hell-hole. It's too hot, the windows don't actually open and, in the unlikely event that I do drop off, someone else starts mithering or moaning, or a baby starts squealing. It's mayhem and I want to go home. I'm so tired I'm not entirely sure I'll survive. I suggest this to LSH and then burst into wracking, uncontrollable sobs. LSH looks worried – not about being left alone with the baby but being left alone with me. I can tell by the way he's looking at me and smiling carefully that he thinks I've taken a step closer to madness. I try to allay his fears between bouts of sobbing and snottering all over the place, but I suspect the fish-knife and pint of water debacles are still too fresh in his mind.

The whole nappy-practising technique was a complete waste of time. Teddies don't squirm, kick and cry. And let's be frank, you don't give a shit if you drop the teddy, do you? Babies, on the other hand, are scary wee wobbly things with legs like rabbits and tiny, tiny extremities which all seem to come to life when unwrapped.

Have been peed on twice today. Dr M left that out as well. Guess a book covering what happens *after* the birth too might have been a good idea.

17 November

Leaving to go home. Yippee! Before we leave we have to dress Louis. God, all the clothes we bought must be for a two-year-old! Have another bout of hysteria. Finally get his wee wobbly arms and legs into the sleep-suit, during which I think his head's going to fall off. Their necks don't work for ages, apparently. I wish someone had told me! By the time he's in the sleep-suit, I can't see him.

Dave drives the car round to the front of the hospital and I walk as slowly as I can – which is also as fast as I can due to the stitches – with Louis in the car seat so as not to jiggle him. It takes us about ten minutes to get the car seat in and then Dave and I get in. I sit in the back to watch Louis. Even starting the engine causes his head to wiggle. Dave drives at about 15 m.p.h. all the way home, only stopping twice. Why didn't I get a manual for this bit?

Arriving home is surreal. It's only been a few days since we were last here and yet we're completely changed. As the front door closes and we look around, I suddenly realise this little tiny bundle is our child and, from here on in, it's up to us. I've never been so overwhelmed with a realisation in my life. There's no buzzer to push if we don't know what we're doing, no efficient-looking people in white uniforms with cheery smiles and a capable way of looking at things. Oh no. It's now David and me . . . alone in the house . . . with a baby.

I've imagined this scene a thousand times – coming home with the baby, smiling, laughing, pouring a Bacardi and Coke and settling down to phone some friends to tell them our glad tidings. I'd ask them over for lunch in a day or two, feed the baby, put him into his cot and go on up to bed myself. Then they'd all arrive the next day with balloons and presents, admire the sleeping child and we'd sit and exchange gossip. There's no room in my fantastic imagination for a huge, exhausted woman walking like John Wayne, wondering what the hell has just happened and unable to relax or sleep for fear that the baby'll just stop breathing there and then. How on earth can such a tiny person survive the reality of living in a house with two people who know absolutely nothing about anything to do with babies? Why did no one tell me? I can't handle this. I don't know what to do! I've had dogs all my life – puppies, rescue dogs and Bone Dog. Poor Bone Dog, now relegated to the kitchen 'cos of potential jealousy and germs. Yes, I've looked after quadrupeds for years without so much as a by-your-leave, but who would've thought a two-legged, 6 lb human baby could reduce me to an insecure, paranoid, clumsy, useless oaf?

Where're we supposed to put him? Does he stay in bed all day? Do we just leave him there on his own? At a complete loss, we take turns holding him and putting him down in the cot till it's bath time. Oh no! Dave and I eye each other up.

He fills the baby bath. We fall out about the temperature. Too hot versus too cold. We lie Louis on a towel, take his clothes off and then toss to see who does the business. Dave loses. It's his call. He picks this wee rabbity-legged baby up in the crook of his arm and gently – 'Watch his head! Watch his head!' – lowers him into the water. He just lies there staring up. Good. At least he doesn't cry. As Dave holds him, I wash him gently and we then lift him back out again, relieved not to have drowned him. By the time he's back in a nappy and sleep-suit, we exhale loudly. The whole thing is so damn complicated – the responsibility too much to bear. We settle down for the night.

18 November
2.30 a.m.

And another thing. Why call night 'night'? Up constantly all day and all night with the baby feeding.

'The baby will need to feed approximately every four hours.' Four hours my arse. Two hours tops. *Tops!* Can you imagine how tired I am?

9.30 a.m.

Community midwife arrives and asks how I am. Fine, I lie. Could I have told her the truth? Could I have asked her if this is night or day? It's dark all the time anyway. But no joke – this isn't funny. We haven't got a clue. If he cries, I want to phone my mum; if he's asleep, I want to wake him up to check that he *is* just asleep. If he has a blanket on, I think he's too hot and whip it off. Once I've whipped it off, I fret that he's too cold and wrap him up again.

Look up Dr M but there's no more – no more instructions, no more helpful tips and photographs against which you can measure yourself or your baby or your husband or the size of your enormous arse. *Oh – my – God!* How did this happen? We're alone. HELP!

Choose not to go down this route with the midwife for fear she phones Social Services, puts me in an institution and gets Louis adopted by people who know what the hell they're doing and are qualified to be parents.

Oh – and the three sleep-suits that Dr M suggested we buy are all far too big. Wee Louis was not even 7 pounds when he was born but, due to the fact I was officially the size of a planet, I thought he was going to be huge. Everyone told me as they scrutinised my tummy with half-shut eyes, 'Yup, that's a big baby all right.' Bullshit! He was only 6 lb 13 oz, so quite where the other 4 stone sprang from I've no idea.

As a result of this miscalculation, it seems that Louis is destined to start life in cast-offs from my teddy. The funny, knitted, knobbly clothes I wore when I was tiny – handed down to my inanimate, glass-eyed bear – are now his. He looks quite fetching, although I hope the long-term mental health of my beloved child is not in danger as it's a seersucker tartan dress that fits best.

19 November

The midwife's back again.

'OK today?'

I nod with my fake grin in place.

I'm supposed to be in love with child by this time, I think. But the fact is I'm too scared of him to be in love with him. What's the point in getting too attached when I'm clearly going to drop him, smother him or drown him by mistake over the next few days? How can this baby survive having me as a mother?

10.45 a.m.
As I gaze at Louis, I suddenly notice he has a throbbing bit towards the front of his head. What the hell is that? I reach for the phone and call my pal, trying not to panic.

'Remember those big, baldy-brain-head aliens in *Star Trek* whose heads went in and out as they breathed,' I ask?

'Yes,' she says.

'Well, I think Louis is one.'

She soon tells me that it's perfectly normal. It's called his fontanelle and it's a soft part on his head where you do see the heartbeat until the skull hardens up. For a moment I feel better and then I begin to worry that a slight poke in the wrong place may prove fatal. Wonder about the practicalities of getting a small, customised helmet made for him, but she tells me to calm down as every child has one. Phew!

20 November
9.45 a.m.
Midwife comes round again. Can tell by the look in her eye that she thinks we've been burgled.

'We haven't,' I explain, trying to smile, 'we're just a bit disorganised.' It's hard to smile when you've had ten minutes' sleep.

She's direct. 'On the bed. Let's see your stitches.' Well, what a silver-tongued little darling, I think as I lumber over, hoist up my nightie and lie there in my own bedroom thinking fondly of the last time there'd been any nightie-hoisting in these parts. It wasn't quite like this, I muse, as she unfurls her rubbery glove, slips it on and starts prodding and probing around my swollen underparts – and just as well, I can tell you. It's blooming sore and humiliating, and heroically I resist the urge to kick her hard in the head.

I've nothing much to say having lost the power of speech, so she's soon on her way – leaving us alone again. God, why didn't she stay? Do you think she'd move in with us for a while? Maybe just for the first six months?

10.15 a.m.

Dave suggests I go and get some rest – he'll take Louis out for a walk in the pram. A good plan. I go upstairs and lie down trying to sleep. You'd think having had none for a week I'd be out like a light – but no. I can't sleep. I hear the front door going and I watch as Dave pushes the pram down the path and out on to the road – with one hand. I open the window and shout, 'Use two hands, Dave, two hands!' He looks at me and secures the handle with both. He knows I'm a woman on the edge of reason.

21 November

It's dark at three in the afternoon and dark till nine in the morning. There's a very small window of opportunity in which to see daylight. It's so cold I'm afraid the baby will freeze to death if we leave the house. Slump into depression. Go to the loo. I know it's normal to bleed for a while after the birth, but I suddenly pass something that looks like Hartleys strawberry jam – without the seeds. Panic. Heart rate up to 6000 b.p.m. Tell Dave to get the lawyer to write out a draft will – I'm clearly dying.

Phone the doctor. Doctor tells me it's just a wee clot and not to fret. A wee clot and not to fret? Is he mad? Since when do grown women with exhausted smiles have clots flowing willy-nilly from their nether regions? No bugger's told me that either! If you ask me, my book stopped when it gets hard!

22 November

Doctor was right. I've survived.

12.30 p.m.

Huh? Doorbell rings. Aaargh! Uninvited guests. House like a bombsite, head like mince. Open the door. It's the Head of Programmes for Radio Scotland with a bunch of red roses and a bottle of champagne. How very nice, I think – if perhaps a little excessive. I mean, a card would've been ample.

He bursts in, very excited. We made a radio pilot a few months ago to try and secure a slot on Radio 1 but which – due to recent events – I've completely forgotten about. It seems I've got the job – the early-morning breakfast show on Saturdays and Sundays from Glasgow on the national Radio 1 network. It's a dream ticket, a dream job, a once-in-a-lifetime opportunity . . . and I don't think I can do it. Not now. I feel so different. I can't sit down as we open the champagne. I feel sick. I feel panicky. I don't know what to do.

I smile and sip champagne, my heart beating like a drum. Oh dear. He leaves an hour later and I've taken virtually nothing of the conversation in. I can think of nothing other than Louis and I can hear him crying whilst this guy's talking to me. I'm going to have to tell him the truth. I can't do the job now. I just can't.

23 November

Have little time to worry about the Radio 1 job. Up most of the night, with Louis feeding every two hours. Is this normal?

10 a.m.

Phone rings. I pick it up. It's the girls at work.

'Can we come and see the baby?'

'Yes, of course,' I say as confidently as I can, sounding like the old Alison. But, as I glance downwards, I need no reminding that this is not strictly the case. For there I sit, topless on a rubber ring, looking and feeling like Ermintrude the Cow. I'm under no illusion that it's going to take more than a quick spot of lipstick to sort this lot out. In the absence of a plastic surgeon, I have to attempt the sorely needed overhaul myself. But it'll take time – and lots of it – so I draft Mum in to help. She's down from Aberdeen and coming round at ten tomorrow morning.

I swear that, if a week ago someone had told me I'd be on the phone to my mum asking her to come round to look after the baby just to give me enough time to get washed and dressed, I'd have laughed in their face and told them they were mad and must have mistaken me for someone who allowed their baby to interfere with their routine. Now I know better. It's me that was mad, ignorant and unrealistic. Nothing is the same.

24 November
14 stone 2 pounds

Have had about three hours sleep. Look and feel shocking. Louis seems fine but, to be honest, I don't think I'd know any different if he wasn't. Why don't kids come with an instruction manual? In our case, I suspect this trial-and-error business is more error. I let him sleep in the bed. Apart from the fact he seems to want to eat almost constantly and I can barely whip up the energy to get up and put him in his wee cot, I just can't bear the thought of his wee, warm, snuggled-up body in a cold Moses basket all on his own with no one to cuddle him. This is commonly known as a rod for my own back and I've chosen not to mention it to the midwife or anyone else.

Back to the job in hand. The pressure is on. My child-free work colleagues are due at midday and I'm determined to appear in control and relaxed, despite the reality of the situation.

10 a.m.

Mum arrives.

'Why didn't you tell me?' I ask, answering the door in my baggy night-shirt, hair on end, eyes like roadmaps. She needs no explanation as to what I'm referring.

'Well, if I'd told you, you'd never have done it,' she answers.

True. So off I go to have a good dig around in my wardrobe.

I'm in no mood to be slow and methodical – actually, I was never in the mood to be slow and methodical – so one by one I grab all my clothes and fling them on to the bed. I'll have a good look through them once I've had a shower and washed my hair.

After a good ten minutes standing under the water, I do feel better – almost human, in fact – until, as I lumber back through to the bedroom, I make the heinous mistake of looking at my reflection in my dressing-table mirror. I can't believe my eyes. As far as I can remember, I've had the baby. A cursory look round the bedroom at the piles of clothes and nappies confirms this to be true. So why in God's name do I look as if I'm still carrying triplets in my gigantic belly? Moving up – only by about an inch – and there are my tits. My God, these aren't mine! Mine have a shape and look like – well – like tits, but these! God, these are indescribably huge.

Holding back the tears, I put on my non-supportive G-string bra – which is better than nothing but only because it helps me punctuate where my chest ends and my gigantic over-hanging splat of a belly begins – and, once secured, put on the gigantic pants and idly wonder if Michelle Pfieffer has ever felt like this. I suspect not as I begin the trial of trying to find some creation to wear from all the clothes strewn over the bed.

None of them fit – not one shirt, one pair of trousers or one dress. Not even the ancient kaftan I've had for about fifteen years and never worn 'cos it's like a bell-tent. (As a last resort I do try it on, but even this won't unravel over my big arse.)

This rapidly brings me to the rather depressing conclusion that I have to climb back into the maternity clothes. God, am I destined to wear the big black trousers and overly bright batik shirts in public once again? It seems so.

It's too depressing to dwell on so instead I concentrate on my hair. Of all the things that have distorted, stretched and changed over the past months, the one thing that has remained the same – thank God – is my hair. It's long and handy to hide under. I make a mental note to phone Derek, my hairdresser, and ask him how long it'll take to grow it to the floor and cover up my maternity slacks. I then apply too much Elizabeth Arden foundation in an attempt to detract from my Demis Roussos-style body shape and check the clock. Good God, it's 11.45. How on earth can it take almost two hours to have a shower, get dressed and dry my hair? How?

If I'm quick, I'll just have time to deflate the rubber ring, hide it under the stairs and shuffle into the kitchen to make a load of sandwiches.

The second I've finished making them, the doorbell rings. God, they're here. A quick glance in the mirror confirms I still look the same from my forehead down to my chin, so hopefully they'll disregard the rest.

12 p.m.

I open the door and can't believe my eyes. Vertical grown-ups in suits! They all come bustling in with big smiles and big cuddles, pushing past me to see the baby. I point them in the direction of the lounge where Mum – bless her – has got Louis looking all pink, powdered and delightful. And as I watch, one of them briefly coos over him as the other two give him a superficial prod with their polished red fingernails before sitting down to be waited on hand and foot.

I can't believe it! Was I really one of these people – these people who go out into the big wide world, wear high heels and look efficient and in control? I must have been and, in twelve weeks' time, I know I'll have to be once again. I'll be fine by then, I think, as I put down the plates of sandwiches and offer them all a drink.

'Tea? Coffee? Wine?'

'Gin and tonic?' one of them asks.

'Sure,' I say, as I rush through to the kitchen to the empty fridge and, for the first time since I was sixteen, a virtually empty booze cabinet.

Ten minutes later we all have drinks and, after a two-minute conversation about Louis, everyone begins chatting about work. Everyone except me, that is. I can't quite take it in. I look the same (bar the extra four stone) but I feel so completely different. Completely. The ins and outs of day-to-day life at work are a different world and, as I look at my wee squishy baby who's still being held by Mum, I notice with a near tear in my eye that not one of the girls feels brave or maternal enough to hold him. And I wonder if I'll ever be one of them again.

I dip in and out of their chat but feel very much on the periphery of what they're discussing. Who gives a flying f*** about all that inconsequential bullshit? Have they not noticed there's a new and fabulous life in the room? Do they not want to acknowledge the miracle of life that has emerged from me? The miracle who, by the way, is now looking especially cute in a tartan seersucker dress? Apparently not. To make matters worse, Louis starts grizzling so I pick him up and jiggle him about rather vigorously as I struggle to keep hold of the thread of conversation buzzing around me. As my frustration grows at not being able to concentrate on what on earth they're talking about, my jiggling technique is pushed to the limit. Now I can't converse with my old friends or keep my baby quiet, so where exactly do I fit in? Oh, that's right, I don't.

It's just as I've come to this particularly disturbing conclusion that Louis opens his mouth and out of it shoots what is commonly known as projectile vomit. It spurts all over the table, all over the sandwiches, all over me, the carpet and the dog. The three working girls leap to their feet in horror.

'Would you like a hand?' one of the braver ones asks.

'Oh no, I'll be all right. I'm fine,' I lie.

The relief on her face is palpable as one of the less brave ones pipes up, 'Och, well, we should be going really and let you get on.' And before I can say, 'It won't take me a minute to ditch the vomit-encrusted sandwiches and make a new batch,' they're standing up and filing out of the door, heels clicking as they go. They can't get away fast enough. I wave goodbye – smiling as best I can – shut the door behind them and burst into tears.

30 November

Have had so little sleep I can't function. By the time I get Louis up, changed, fed and dressed, and then have a shower and get dressed myself, it's almost dark again. I bloody hate Scotland at this time of year. There's no natural light at all. Bloody miserable.

31 November

Every night between midnight and 2 a.m. Louis cries. It doesn't matter what I do or how I do it, he just opens his small, perfectly formed mouth and exercises his small, perfectly formed lungs. It cuts through me like a cheesewire, I swear – rips right through my body and squeezes my heart. What can I do? I can't help him – his little red face all screwed up and wet and his stomach like a washboard. I've been told it's colic. We can send people to the moon, we can speak to people on the other side of the world at the touch of a button. But there is no known cure for colic. I bet if men had babies, we'd have a cure for it

– as well as pain-free childbirth. And if that *was* the case, the chances are nobody would've bothered sending any poor sod to the moon!

1 December

Get some stuff to help colic. Wait till the evening, when Louis is howling and his mouth's open, and grab the stuff. I've no idea how you're supposed to put anything into a baby's mouth that isn't my chest. Eventually just go for the squirt-it-in method – from this point forever to be known as the 'ill-advised squirt-it-in method', as the entire contents of his stomach instantly shoot out all over him, me and the bed. On the bright side, though, it seems that shock cures colic as well.

2 December

I've never smelled a baby before. I haven't. It's a smell like no other and I just absolutely love it. I love the smell of his head, his neck, the creases behind his knees, his wee innocent baby mouth, his ears . . . In fact, I could just lie around all day smelling him. I inhale. Mmmm.

4 December

Another thing I didn't know about is the regularity with which you have to change nappies. Naively, I thought a couple of times a day would do it, but these wee human people seem to spend most of the day and night with things flying out of one orifice or another. My nappy-changing technique is improving and it's now dawning on me that an entire table for changing a baby on is just a rip-off. A mat on the floor, a towel on the floor, the floor – but why have a £300 Mamas & Papas pine dresser with a flat top, for God's sake? Every chest of drawers in the world has a flat top, every home has a flat floor. Yes, another useless piece of equipment we were bamboozled into buying.

6 December

Phone up and turn down the Radio 1 job. I have to. I've spoken to my pal Sarah about the dilemma I face. The thought of doing *anything* is too overwhelming, but the idea of leaving this helpless wee bundle whilst I go off and entertain the world just seems impossible right now.

'You have a choice,' she told me. 'You have a career before children, and afterwards you have a job. If you choose to have a career, that's great, but remember that your priority will not be the baby, it'll be work, and remember that you'll have to do it 100 per cent or not at all.' Right now it's exactly how I feel. Decision made. I phone and tell Radio Scotland I cannot accept their offer. They're understandably shocked and try to talk me round. It cannot be done. I'm left with a hollow, empty feeling as I replace the receiver. That was the career opportunity of a lifetime, I suspect, and I've just walked away from it.

8 December

Same old sleepless nights, same old baggy bod. Louis is a little angel, though. Every day he seems to change a bit. His eyes squint up at me and he grows. I can't miss this for the world. I really can't.

9 December
13 stone 13 pounds

I've not only fallen in love with my child, I'm now completely obsessed with him. I watch telly, hear stories of a flu sweeping Asia and worry myself sick that it'll hit the UK and that he'll get it and die. There's an outbreak of Legionaires' disease very close to where we live. Are the particles in the air? Will they get into our house and into my wee baby's lungs? There's a docu-mentary about cot death and the latest theory is that it has to do with antimony in mattresses. We look at Louis's mattress. It has antimony in it. We throw it out, despite the fact that he hasn't even slept on it 'cos he's been in our bed from day one. I know the theory is not to have him in bed with us, but, to be honest, he's awake more than asleep so why not just lie there on one side and feed him rather than marching across the room and sitting upright in a chair?

10 December

Jeffy's son Lyle's first birthday party. It used to be a breeze leaving the house. In fact, I never even thought about it. I'd just grab my keys and run out the door. How I wish I'd appreciated such a simple thing. Now it takes hours. Hours. Today, after I've showered and wrestled my hugeness into some clothes for the first time in a long time, I put on some make-up. That's the easy part. The next bit takes ages – getting Louis up, washed, changed, fed, dressed and ultimately wrapped in a huge cosy suit as it's blooming freezing outside. I then check I have everything I might need for him jammed in the bag – nappies, wipes, cream for his bottom, bib, rattle – and, by the time we're ready to go, I'm exhausted. It takes another couple of minutes to fit him into his car seat and then the car and finally we're off.

Arriving in a flat full of other mothers is wonderful to begin with. The only real problem is that they all look as though they're in control. And, in comparison to me, they are. They walk, they talk and they interact with one another. I even hear laughter. I swear, I do.

We stay for a couple of hours. I sit in a corner hoping no one will come and talk to Louis as there are so many germs around

I'm convinced he'll get some virus or other which will almost certainly kill him. So there I sit, just looking around with a glazed expression, taking nothing in.

I don't feel like I belong anywhere anymore. I'm no longer the carefree DJ chick with the huge capacity for lager and bawdy jokes. Nor am I a calm, serene earth mother who just sits back and lets everything wash over her. No, I'm a neurotic balloon terrified to go anywhere and do anything as I'm not responsible or mature enough to look after this child. He deserves better. He deserves someone who knows what they're doing; someone who can decipher the noises he makes and what they mean; someone who isn't too scared to pick him up in case they hurt him; someone who doesn't need to stay awake all night to check that he's still breathing; someone who knows about these sorts of things – these *baby* things. Surely someone *must* have an instruction manual?

11 December
Virtually no sleep at all – just the endless night after the endless day of feeding and dozing, and all in the dark. I must remember to emigrate when I feel better.

One month old

13 December
The reality of being so isolated has hit home now. David is very busy with the restaurant and I'm stranded on my own in *Terry and June* land with Louis and Mullet. It seems my details were lost during our house move and so I didn't get the chance to attend an antenatal class in the area. This means I've no one to share things with. Wish I'd stuck in at the NCT classes now. At least all those Davids and Alisons would be around for a bit

of a chat. My non-baby friends won't want to hear about all this and my baby ones' children are much older anyway, so they've mostly gone back to work. As for the neighbours? Well, there's no one of our generation. They're all lovely but the average age is about sixty-five. Don't quite know what to do about that. Too tired to do anything just now, that's for sure.

16: December

My pal James comes round. James has a sister and nephew and nieces so can probably gauge the situation very well: out-of-control woman with tiny baby. I'm putting on a brave face, however, as we sit and chat. Louis grizzles and needs feeding so I get my boob out – quite subtly, a trick I've been perfecting. The idea is that, rather than unbuttoning my whole shirt and sitting there like Jordan in the back of a taxi after a good night out, I just undo one or two buttons, fiddle round with the scaffolding bra underneath until I release one of my monster tits and – hey presto! – the baby is feeding.

James and I are chatting whilst Louis feeds. But then, when Louis stops suckling, I notice James's expression changes from one of practised indifference to one of eye-popping horror. Following his gaze, I understand why. There's a generous arc of milk spraying with an impressive trajectory from my nipple and landing on the carpet between us. I try and cover it up with some bonhomie as I fumble around, wrestling my boob into its casing and wondering if I may be milked to death, but inside I'm dying of embarrassment. I mean, *dying*.

After James has left – quickly – I sit down and look at Louis. He in turn looks right back at me. Really *looks* – no blinking, no diversion, just a good stare. I let his gaze go, stand up and walk away and his head follows me – his head lifted off the back of his bouncy chair at about 45 degrees and he *watches* me. Maybe he thinks I'm going to leg it.

17 December

Just in the house today, smelling the baby. Yum, yum!

18 December

One week till Christmas. We put up a tree. The lights are on but nobody's home.

20 December

13 stone 11 pounds

Radio station's Christmas party. Don't feel like going. I look and feel hellish. Still no sleep, still no clothes other than huge, baggy, flappy things, but make the effort – determined to show the world I'm the same. I'm not. Last year I went out, had a meal and stood my hand at the bar for three hours before climbing on to the stage and singing with the band. Later on I had a two-hour conversation in the gents' loo with one of my friends and the next thing I knew I was waking up at 8.30 a.m. in the communal stair of our flat. Our neighbours must have stepped over me to get to work. This was a defining moment – defining me as a revolting drunk. Allegedly, I'd leant against the buzzer 'cos I couldn't get my key in the lock and LSH had come running down thinking I was being attacked. When I saw his face, I smiled, and when he saw mine, he turned on his heel and went straight back up to bed. Not amused, understandably. Had the boot been on the other foot, I'd have killed him. Still, none of that this year – oh no! By way of slight contrast, this year's party consists more of a pizza, a hot flush, a leaking right breast and a taxi home before the band even starts. I feel like I don't belong anywhere any more.

23 December

Shit! Haven't done any Christmas shopping. Haven't slept for months either. This must be the hungriest baby in the world. Every two hours, day and night, he's hungry. Lucky he's also the cutest, most gorgeous thing I've ever seen in my life.

So knackered, I can't speak let alone shop. God, why am I not like these elfin super-mums who snap back into shape, into their jeans and into their lives in a fortnight? Here I am, coming on for six weeks after the baby arrived and still in a complete bloody shambles.

Mum and Dad are having Christmas at theirs, which is great. This means all David and I need to do is drive 130 miles north to Aberdeen. Phew!

24 December

Did I say '*all* we have to do'? God, it's not a Volvo *estate* and we barely have enough room for everything we need: the pram, the bath, the changing mat, the nappies, the array of interesting dangly things he can lie under, the changing bag, the car seat and the very pissed-off and generally ignored dog, who has slipped from number one citizen to kitchen dweller with bad breath and a sad eye. Would feel guilty if I'd the energy for guilt, but have to expend too much energy just staying awake.

The car is packed to the gunnels and we're ready to go. Even before we hit the Forth Road Bridge we have to stop. Louis is squealing his wee lungs out. It's pouring with rain and there's a good gale blowing. I wrestle him out of the car seat, take him into the front, grapple around, get my boob out and sit there feeding him. He has a good snack for ten minutes and then, after a further five minutes' farting about, we're on the road again.

Just as we reach the other end of the Forth Road Bridge, Bone Dog barks. He needs out.

'Did you put him out before we left?' I ask.

'I was too bloody busy packing the car,' says Dave. 'Did you?'
I shake my head. We know Bone Dog's history in the back of
cars only too well and, while the golf clubs and bag scenario was
bad enough, if he loses it here with all the baby paraphernalia
packed round him, I'll be forced to ship him back from whence
he came. So we stop again – this time for Bone Dog, who has
to be wrestled out from under a suitcase, baby bath and pram.
Frustratingly, he just stands at the side of the road – his long
mane of black fur blowing wildly around his depressed face –
and does nothing. I think he's making a point.

25 December

Merry Christmas. I hear the music, see the tree and sit propped
up with a mince pie and flagon of wine as Dave tries to work
the video camera. But try as I might, I just can't whip up the
Christmas spirit on three hours' sleep.

When we start opening our presents, Louis starts grizzling. I
howk up my dressing-gown and wrestle one of my boobs out.
It's getting bigger, I'm convinced. Is that possible? It really
should be named, christened and introduced to people as its
own entity, really it should. I could dress it in fashionable
scarves and things.

As it eventually appears Zeppelin-like from my nightie, I
notice my dad stand up, cough and say, 'Eh, I'm just off to put
the rubbish out.' Now, this may sound like a reasonable sort of
thing for your father to say, but not mine. He's not a man prone
to jumping up out of his Parker Knoll recliner on Christmas
morning and just putting rubbish out willy-nilly. Even my own
dad is scared of my gigantic breast. And who can blame him? I
remember only too well seeing Jim Dale and Digby, the Biggest
Dog in the World. Anything that oversized and uncontrollable
is scary. At least Digby had a face.

26: December

Boxing Day. Maybe it's called this 'cos at this stage, six weeks after having a baby, you feel like you've done twelve rounds with Mike Tyson and Mohammed Ali. Actually, they wouldn't be able to get near me for these boobs, which – incidentally – are now throbbing.

27 December

Feel very feverish. Hope to God it's not the flu.

28 December

No, it's not the flu, I've got mastitis. Great. This is a thing that happens to boobs. They go all hard, there's too much milk in them and they heat up – and you just wish they weren't attached to your body. Turning a hot shower on to them can help – I tried – but the classic solution is to get a cabbage, peel off the outer leaves, put them in the freezer and then sit with them round your boobs. No, I can't believe it either. Not only do I feel like a vegetable, but it seems as if I'm literally turning into one now. Cabbage in my shirt, cabbage in my head.

31 December

Aim to leave early. By the time we repack the car it's almost lunchtime. Arrive back in Edinburgh and take the rest of the day to empty the car. We're used to lugging things around on Hogmanay – usually crates of beer and boxes of food – and then journeying into the country to spend a few wild nights and days with friends. This is a new and different experience altogether.

10. p.m.

LSH and I are in bed. Bed at 10 p.m.! This is New Year's Eve and we're the pair who only one year ago danced till dawn, sang songs, drank whisky and partied all night long. Who'd have thought it?

1 January
1 a.m.

The phone rings. 'Happy New Year!' It's our friends, who are all in Braemar, plastered and dancing in some hotel. We speak to them all one by one – all slurring, all laughing – and we're even made to speak to a Great Dane called Ruby. Having had enough by then, I just shout, 'Walkies!' instead and all I can hear is the dog starting to bark and knock things over as it thinks it's going out. We have a laugh and then I begin to cry. How sad am I? Officially now jealous of an oversized dog with bad breath and an eight-year lifespan. Try to go back to sleep.

2 a.m.

Louis awakes for a feed to find me lying there mourning my old life. As my self-pity hits an all-time revolting high Louis, my wee pudding, looks me straight in the eye, gurgles and gives me the biggest, best, most gummy smile I've ever seen in my life. I'm in love. It's true. He's fab. It's as if he's saying, 'Hang on in there, Mum, *I* love you.' Bugger wine, men and song. It's all worth it.

3 a.m.

Still awake. Only person in the house awake. Feel a bit mad.

4 a.m.

Still a-bloody-wake. Only person in the country awake. Rephrase that. Only *sober* person in the country awake.

5 a.m.

Right! No point in lying here like a sack of tatties.

I quite fancy a cup of hot chocolate, so I get up. Don't put on the light so as not to disturb Dave and Louis, which is how I come to trip over the discarded sausage-shaped cushion, fly forward and bang my nose off the side of the wardrobe. I even knock myself out for a moment.

When I come round again, I'm on my knees in front of the wardrobe and there are copious amounts of blood coming from my nostrils. I may have broken my nose.

6.45 a.m.

Here we are, sitting in the car park outside the casualty department with tissues padding my very sore nose. Which is bad enough, but add to it the fact that the ground is frozen, it's pitch dark and my right mammary is out and being attacked by a small boy and – just to complete the scene of fun and frivolity – there's a waiting-room full of New Year revellers linking arms and singing 'Auld Lang Syne'. To say I'm not in high spirits doesn't quite hit the mark. Dave goes in and registers me as I sit hiding in my blood-spattered dressing-gown and look on as normal people, unaware of the mayhem and madness that sits in this battered old Volvo, go on their merry way.

9.15 a.m.

Doctor says it's not broken, just badly bruised. No instructions other than an icepack and to see my own doctor in about a week just to check. I need no excuses to stay in the house. It's cold, it's dark, I look like I've been punched in the face by a large professional boxer and I'm thoroughly knackered.

3 January

Jeffy and Chris come round to first-foot us. They're horrified to

ALISON'S DIARY

see my bruised and swollen face. I tell them I'm a victim of
domestic violence – I was hit by a wardrobe. The severe black-
and-blue effect is fading somewhat and the general hue I'm now
modelling is more yellow and purple.

7 January

Go to GP who looks at my nose. The swelling has gone down
considerably so he says it's OK as he looks at my notes. Whilst
I'm in, he suggests we do the six-week check.

'Six-week check?' I ask naïvely. 'Sure, what's that then?' Well,
blow me if that doesn't consist of whipping my knickers off and
letting him explore my inner sanctum with a variety of alien
instruments. God, no wonder my nose begins to bleed again.

Stumble out with red nose and matching red face. Phone
Dave and suggest we go to the pub. He points out that it's only
9.30 in the morning.

'I bloody know that,' I shout, 'I need a drink!' We go home
and I have a Bacardi and Coke. Bugger it!

12 p.m.

Wake up. I'm out of practice. One large rum and Coke and no
sleep and I'm out like a light. Feel much better for it. Louis is
happy, I'm happy, Dave is still here so he can't be too bloody
unhappy.

8 January

Phone a few friends and berate them for not warning me about
the six-week check. Feel considerably better when my pal Kim
tells a story about a six-week check. As the woman sat in the
doctor's waiting-room, she became a bit paranoid about what
was going on down below so slunk off to the loo to have a wee
wash and dry with a hanky before her appointment. She was

duly called in and, as she lay there – legs akimbo and thinking of killing her husband – the doctor took a cursory look at her nether regions and looked puzzled before walking briskly to his desk and picking up a pair of tweezers. Closing her eyes tightly, she suspected there was about to be a degree of pain coming her way for whatever reason and was rather surprised when he deftly leaned forward and plucked a postage stamp from her fanny! Clearly it had been wrapped up in the hanky.

I send Kim a roll of pre-stuck stamps and suggest that at least she remembers to stick to the traditional method of licking them . . . with her tongue!

10 January

Every day is the same just now. It consists of Louis still feeding every two hours. I'm so damn tired, I don't know what time of day it is. My body is the same shape as it was before I had him and I'd dearly like to go on a diet but can't stop eating. I'm ravenous. I've taken to carrying bananas around in my handbag and car so that there is always one to hand, and I'm devouring them with such regularity I wonder if I'm sliding back down the food chain.

11 January
5 a.m.

It suddenly dawns on me that this is it. This is not going to stop. This aching tiredness will not end. I'll not suddenly be sent to Benidorm for a two-week holiday to drink Sangria and recharge my batteries. What a revelation – or perhaps 'deflation' is a more appropriate word.

As I lie here contemplating my life, Louis wakes up, looks right at me and laughs. He actually laughs. Dashing around later I look up my Milestone Chart and it seems that – yes – babies will laugh and smile from two months of age. Wow! I thought they just lay in bed for about a year doing nothing! What a clever lad, I think, until I consider the context of his laugh – me slumped and panicking in bed at 5 in the morning. There's no doubt he has Mackie blood in him from my mother's side of the family. They always laugh at someone else's misfortune – in this case, mine.

Two months old

14 January

Definition of sleep: a natural recurring condition of suspended consciousness by which the body rests. Ha, ha, ha!

If I was a spy and had sworn my allegiance to the Queen and to die with my state secrets, I'd now have to spill the beans. This lack of sleep is torture – no more, no less. *Hell – on – earth.* My eyes are always half-shut, my brain has shut down, I look like a baggy-eyed monster and my temper is short. The only one who receives my loving gaze at the moment is wee Louis, who is happily oblivious of what he's doing to this person who used to be called Alison and who once had vaguely human characteristics.

Have also noticed that when people speak to me, I see their lips moving, hear the words but take none of it in at all. I can drift off into a zombie-like state in a second. Sometimes, when I ask a question, I've forgotten what I asked by the time they're halfway through the answer. This is not the sign of an intelligent human being, this is the sign of a blancmange.

10 a.m.

Off to the doctor for Louis's first inoculation. Diptheria, tetanus and polio. How can they do this to such a small, innocent, gentle wee toots? I've read about it in a pamphlet – which warns that there might be a reaction – and I've got myself in a state about it. Really, women have babies in bushes and it seems I can't do the most straightforward, practical thing without going to pieces.

Put on a brave face, go into the consulting-room, see the needle and burst into tears. As predicted, there was a reaction – mine. Hardly a tower of strength, I go to the loo, splash my face with cold water and gamely hold Louis's tiny wee arm as the doctor jabs him with this gigantic needle. Louis is fine – bar a five-second outburst – and smiles through the entire experience. Doctor tells me to keep an eye on him – give him some Calpol and watch that he doesn't get too hot. He must recognise a mad look in my eye 'cos then he asks if I've been crying a lot.

'Yes, actually,' I say, crying.

'Do you think you may be a bit down in the dumps?' he asks. I shrug my shoulders and the wobbly lips make a reappearance. 'Well, just keep a check on it and, if you don't perk up, come back and see me,' he suggests.

15 January
3 a.m.

I wonder how many other people are up at this time of night? When I say 'up', I mean 'awake'. When I say 'awake', I mean that my eyes are shut, my baby is feeding, my body is lying in a sort of dislocated way abandoned across the bed but my good old brain is definitely awake.

Lying here on my side with my great glut of a belly spreading out in front of me I'm hardly the most attractive sight to behold. I remember when Dave and I first got married. 'We'll never wear pyjamas,' we announced, leaping into bed for the third time that day. So here I am now in a sort of Wee Willie Winkie bell-tent – blue-and-white brushed cotton, the sort of thing Dot from *EastEnders* would wear, the only difference being that she'd look more fetching in it.

Louis soon drops off to sleep again. I must make the effort to get him into his cot.

16 January

Enough is enough. The decision has been made. Tonight Louis is going into his cot. I feed him, put him down and all's well. In fact, he remains sound asleep until about ten minutes after I get to sleep, when he wakes up. Stumbling across the carpet, I hoist him up, take him over to our bed, lie down briefly to feed him and, when I wake up again, it's morning and Louis is still in the bed. God, the Nazi nanny regime has gone to pot. If the never-have-the-child-sleeping-in-the-bed manual is serious, then it should come with some sort of electrocution device that zaps you awake after you've fallen back into a deep sleep having wrestled the child from the cot to give it a top-up. I feel guilty that he's in the bed, but the bottom line is I really don't care. Burn the bloody book – sleep is precious, sleep is great and, no matter what it takes to get some, I'll do it.

17 January

Can't find the walk-about phone this morning. It's driving me mad. Turn the place upside-down.

12.30 p.m.

Find it – in the fridge. I must've put the milk somewhere else. I wonder if this is tiredness or early Alzheimer's. As my mum says, it doesn't run in our family, it gallops. I suspect it's just galloped up a generation or two and got me.

18 January

Gordon – bless his little acrylic socks – is coming down from

Aberdeen to see Louis. He's my oldest pal and was going to be my bridesmaid until Dave pointed out that the bridesmaid usually stays with the bride on the night before the wedding – which would, under the circumstances, be rather inappropriate. Warn him that I won't be going out doing lager-drinking – our favourite pastime for years – but he says he's not bothered, so we'll look forward to seeing him tomorrow.

19 January

Gordon arrives. Great to see him. He's a natural with babies and, as he sits cradling Louis in his arms, his male biological clock starts ticking.

Gazing at Louis and smiling, with a big soft look in his eyes, he says, 'I'd really like one of these.' I tell him that if I was a bloke, I'd have ten, and encourage him to get on with it – before gently suggesting he may need to find a girlfriend first. He takes this on board as I take Louis off upstairs for a feed. Although I've known Gordon for fifteen years, he's still a complete lad and I don't want his eyes falling out if I get my gino-boobs out. I once had a suspected lump in my breast and Gordon's dad, who's a surgeon in Aberdeen, checked it out for me. It was all fine and eventually I told Gordon about it – who promptly went home and asked his dad what my boobs were like! Yes, he got a thick ear and yes, he's an acquired taste.

Make a big effort to sit up late and chat. By 11 I've had it and take to my bed.

20 January

Think I might venture into town but I only had about ten minutes' sleep last night. Can't believe my ears when David suggests to Gordon that they go out and have a game of golf and then a few drinks. I bite my tongue. I'm being unreasonable.

Why shouldn't they go out and enjoy themselves. Why shouldn't they go out and enjoy themselves? Are you *mad*? Why should I sit demented on my own in the house? I take a deep breath, try to be calm and go upstairs.

Dave comes up in a wee while to get changed and I let rip in a highly irrational way.

'Go out for a drink with *my friend*? He's come down to see me too! I want to go out, it's not fair. I don't want to be left here!' And then, out of nowhere, my twelve-year-old self rears up from my subconscious. 'Anyway, he was *my* friend before he was *yours!*' Sob, sob, boo-hoo!

With my spleen vented and tear ducts emptied, I go off to the loo to repair myself before going back downstairs. Entering the lounge, I see a very sheepish-looking Gordon, who just looks at me and says, 'Alison, the baby monitor's on.' Oops. I'm speechless and then I look at him and we burst out laughing. Gordon goes out and buys us all a takeaway curry. An excellent plan all round.

21 January

Had eight minutes' sleep last night. Clearly lamb rogan josh doesn't agree with Louis, who is up most of the night bawling his wee eyes out. It isn't till early this morning that he bawls his bottom out too, which is definite glow-in-the dark material, direct from *The Far Pavilions*. Better lay off the hot curry for a while.

Bid farewell to Gordon who, despite seeing his pal as a sobbing, overweight, unreasonable hormone-surfer, has vowed to go home and get himself a woman. He wants children now. I'd normally make a joke about him having this one, but I haven't got the energy. Off he goes back to Aberdeen and back to a life.

25 January

Louis is just feeding more and more. He's growing well. Wonder briefly if I can just start him on a little sirloin steak.

He's feeding constantly – all day and all night. It's barely worth putting my boobs away, but put them away I do – mainly 'cos I still can't quite believe they're attached to me. Quite upsetting really.

There's a news item about meningitis on the telly. What a terrifying and devastating disease. Check Louis all over for a rash when bathing him. No, it looks clear. Thank goodness.

27 January

There are a lot of gurgling and cooing sounds now which means that he's becoming much more entertaining. He just lies on his back making strange, underwater-type noises. He seems to recognise my voice now too. If I come into the room and start chatting, he turns round to give me a look and a coo.

29 January

How much is it safe to drink whilst breastfeeding? It seems that there's a degree of debate. Some say one glass, some say none and some just say revert to normal. I'm going to stick to a glass or two, I think, primarily because my tolerance to the great god alcohol has decreased dramatically since he was born and I'm now what's commonly known as a cheap date. Two glasses of wine and I'm three sheets to the wind. Dave reckons this should dramatically decrease our outgoings. Cheeky bugger.

1 February
13 stone 10 pounds

We must be doing something right. Louis is growing steadily

and putting on weight – so, like his mother already. Quality sleep is a thing of the past. Quality time is a thing of the past. There's a general fog in my head which I can't seem to clear. Everything seems such an effort. Getting up, getting dressed, getting Louis dressed and changed – making food, for goodness' sake. The mere thought of it makes me want to go for a wee lie down.

2 February

Off to the doc for a weighing and measuring session. Thank goodness it's just Louis and not me. I need little reminding of my weights and measures. The doctor gives me the glad tidings that in a few weeks' time I can start to introduce Louis to the joys of real food. He assures me that this should mean that he won't be as hungry and will therefore need less from my bazonga boobs. And this in turn means that: a) I may even get them down to a more manageable size; and b) I can travel a little further afield without the baby and so seriously consider getting a little of my old life back.

10 February

Meet Jeffy for a coffee and she produces photographs that were taken just a few months ago. 'Who is that unlined, fresh-faced person?' I wonder. The answer is – shockingly – me. Yes, when bloated and rubbing far too much lemon oil into my tummy every night, I thought I was fat, revolting and haggard. Well, I didn't have a patch on me now. Just as well the baby loves me as I can't see George Clooney crossing the road to say hello, that's for sure – unless it's to ask if I've lost my way from the old people's home and to offer me a lift back.

Three months old

13 February

Unlucky for some – Louis, as it turns out. Here I am, spending another day doing what I've been doing constantly since 13 November – waking up, feeding the baby, getting up, feeding the baby, getting dressed, dressing the baby, eating breakfast, feeding the baby – and it's only today that I think to myself that I may actually be in what is commonly known as a routine. Feeling rather pleased – having not been renowned for being a routine-type of person before.

I put Louis on the bed, ping off his trousers to change him and go off on the hunt for a nappy. As I whistle and wander around, I suddenly hear a very dull thud from the direction of the bedroom, followed by a blood-curdling scream. With my heart in my mouth, I run through to find Louis lying on his back, red-faced and bawling. He's fallen off the bed. I didn't put him close to the edge, though, so the conclusion is that he has rolled. What a time to do it! But he has – he's learned to roll.

15 February

This development nonsense will have to stop. Not only has he learned to roll and been practising so that he's rolling from side to side, over and over, all over the place, but he's also realised that, if he grabs my hair in his fat little paws and gives it a good yank, he can get a fairly extreme reaction from the woman he'll hopefully one day call Mum. He tangles his wee fist up in my hair so tightly when I'm feeding him this afternoon, I think I'm going to have to get it cut back – my hair, not his fist! The wee monkey's making fast in-roads into the issue of control.

19 February

Friend – who shall remain nameless – comes round to tell me that her mother- and father-in-law are staying with her and her husband for a few days. It's never been a particularly happy relationship and has only deteriorated since she had her little girl. The in-laws visit under the false pretence of helping out, but in reality her mother-in-law does absolutely nothing and her father-in-law just watches the racing on TV. She predicted this and so I'm at a loss as to why she's quite so fraught – which she explains when she asks me for a glass of wine when I offer her a coffee.

I soon understand her need when she tells me that last night her mother- and father-in-law were glued to the telly – as per usual. At 7 p.m. she went upstairs to put her eighteen-month-old daughter to bed and read her a story. Twenty minutes later, just after the baby had dropped off, she was bending over the cot tucking the sleeping child in snugly when her husband arrived back from work. Having not seen his wife in that position for quite some time, he grabbed her from behind and gave her a hug. Before either of them knew what was happening, the hug had developed into more of a fumble, grope and then an unexpected sexual encounter – which largely consisted of the two of them grunting and groaning whilst hopping about and trying to get each other's clothes off. Afterwards they emerged downstairs a little flushed and casually sauntered into the lounge, when the baby grizzled and they heard every little snuffle – clear as day – thanks once again to the ever-alert baby monitor.

'Having sex in front of your in-laws. Bet that got their attention away from *Watchdog*,' I joke.

'Yes,' she agrees briefly. How we laugh.

20 February

I've been thinking about that Bacardi and Coke I had a few weeks back. The billboard on the way to the hospital is in my mind a lot too. It's given me back a taste for alcohol and so I plan to go out with some of the girls this weekend. Yes, the time has come to reintroduce myself to the world. I phone my pal Jeffy and arrange to meet up with her first. She introduces the topic gently, but the bottom line is: spontaneous drinking sessions are a thing of the past. It seems I'll have to plan ahead.

21 February

Having had the low-down, it seems that nothing less than a finely tuned military operation is required to get me out of the door for a few hours of freedom. The first thing I must do is express some milk. This is yet another expression – excuse the pun – that I've heard and I have no idea what it means other than to get some milk from me by means of a machine so that Louis can have some when I go out. Expressing milk sounds so easy – like breathing or blinking. Expressing. Once you've expressed the stuff, you just leave the bottle in the fridge and off you go. A piece of the proverbial.

First things first. I purchase the machine, which is – not to put too fine a point on it – a device that looks like a cow-milker. It doesn't take me long to discover that it *is* a cow-milker! The instrument of torture consists of an empty plastic bottle, attached to the top of which is a strange, transparent rubber suction tip. Mmmm, nice! Looking at the image of the serene and smiling woman on the front of the box, it appears this experience will not only be relaxing but also most enjoyable. But the reality of the situation is that I'm expected to stick that nozzle on to my breast and milk myself. I don't blooming well think so. As I read the instructions, flashbacks fill my mind of every piece of news footage I've ever seen featuring large miserable-looking heifers lined up in vast cowsheds and gazing off into the middle distance as battery-operated devices – just like the one I now hold in my hand – suck, tug and pump at their udders. Surely this is not the only way to do this thing? After staring at the box for at least another ten minutes, I review the options: a) swallow my last iota of self-esteem and just milk myself like Ermintrude the Cow; or b) don't and, as a result, forego a social life and any interaction with other human beings for the foreseeable future.

I open the box. Following the instructions to the letter – including trying to recreate the soporific look on the woman's face (bar the smile – I can't do the smile) – results in absolutely nothing. Not one drop – nothing, *nada, Nicht, rien*. Fresh air. Surely to God it can't be that difficult. I mean, here I sit with these huge breasts full to the brim with milk and can I get any out? Not on your life.

It's at this point I envisage the ice melting in that Bacardi sitting on the bar waiting for me to drink it and start to get desperate. I phone Jeffy, who suggests I have a large gin, sit down, relax and try again. Following her instructions – with the addition of scoffing a large bag of cheese and onion crisps – I sit there squeezing and squishing the nozzle on my boob until it's redder and rawer than ever before. I'm at it a full half-hour – by now accompanied by two large gins – and manage to get about three drops of milk out. It cannot be done. It will not be done.

I burst into tears. I'm a bad mother. I'm a useless parent. Yes, I was the vessel in which Louis was carried, but clearly I'm not equipped to follow the job through. I expect he'll disown me as soon as he's old enough to realise who his mother is. Sob.

David tells me to go out anyway. I need a break and he needs a break – and not from the baby but from me, by the look of it. Tomorrow I shall try again and, regardless of the result, will go out for a couple of hours.

24 February

Have another milking session, but it seems Ermintrude has left the building. Put the machine back in its box and vow to burn it.

I get ready to go out. David is armed with a bottle filled with formula milk, which he has convinced me will not kill our child and will bring me back to life. I've been indoctrinated with the breastfeeding guilt trip practically since Louis was born and the very suggestion of bottle-feeding a baby formula is enough to bring me out in lumps so I haven't even considered it as a possibility. I relent – why am I being so unreasonable? Bloody hormones! And so, after I take an hour to get ready to go out, I give Louis a boobful.

Disappointingly, I'm still looking like a bag of undulating water as I catch sight of myself in the hall mirror before I get into the cab to take me to The Baillie – my favourite bar in the whole world where I'm meeting a few friends. Entering the bar, the first person I see is a bloke I've known for years, who removes his pint from his lips just long enough to say, 'God, you've put on the beef.' I smile weakly and walk past. Where has my razor-sharp tongue gone? Why didn't I make him wither and cringe in front of his friends the way I used to? Because I'm too busy forcing my beefy body through the crowds and into the ladies to find a cubicle for a howl. What is wrong with me? Xena the Warrior Princess has gone and been replaced by a whinging, snivelling fool. Will I ever feel like me again?

I hang back till I can repair myself sufficiently to stroll back through the bar, head down, staring at the ground – or would do if gigantic breasts weren't obscuring my view – then hail a taxi to take me home. Arrive home exactly fifty minutes after I've left.

Louis is crying his heart out. Dave is red-faced and fraught. It seems the bottle has been rejected without so much as a by-your-leave. God. I sit down, get my boobs out and tell Dave about my fun night out. Louis stops crying as I start.

'Never mind,' says LSH, 'I still love you.' Make mental note to get Labrador and white stick for his birthday.

25 February

Wonder if I can get small balls of cotton-wool to plug up my tear ducts. They're overactive and need to be stopped. Adverts for *Yellow Pages* on TV make me howl, even the Dulux paint ad with that big hairy dog sets me off. Watched *Little House on the Prairie* and almost had to be sedated. I must invent small duct-pluggers for all over-emotional postnatal women of this world. Maybe my destiny is to be an inventor.

27 February

The thought of going back to work is filling me with dread. I speak to my boss, who says if I come back now he'll give me a month's salary. This is all I'm offered. I've worked there for four years, but there's no obligation to give me proper maternity pay. The joys of the self-employed. Anyway, the mere thought of going back and working six days a week full on – I just can't do it. Not yet. Not just now. I can't. I don't want to leave my toothless wee pudding with anyone and so I explain this to my boss, who thinks I've lost my mind. He could be right.

28 February

Get a phone call from a guy starting a new radio station, who wants me to go and work for him. I tell him I'm not really in the market, but he perseveres and talks me into at least meeting him. Nothing ventured, I suppose.

1 March

Meet the MD of Scot FM, determined just to have a non-committal chat. An hour later we shake on it. Yes, I've a new job. I'll work two days a week to start with, broadcasting on a Saturday and Sunday lunchtime from their new studio in Edinburgh's Leith. I was initially reluctant, but when they started talking money, I realised these guys are going to put their money where their mouths are and at this stage it'd be foolhardy and utterly stupid to say no.

As soon as I get home, I tell Dave my great news and it quickly dawns on me that I'm so excited and carried away with the job offer that I've completely forgotten I've no childcare lined up at all. Mum and Dad are in Aberdeen, my mother-in-law has just started a new relationship, which is taking up her waking hours, and I've no brothers or sisters. What shall I do? I briefly wish I was Italian, with five sisters flooded with maternal feelings who could look after my wee sausage when I go back to work. Obviously this is a tad unrealistic, so I snap out of it and make a few phone calls instead.

Ask friends how you go about it. Some say adverts, some say word of mouth, some laugh in my face. So I start with a few phone calls. Not one of them even gives me the time of day. It seems the world is full of childminders, most of whom have far more children than they know what to do with. Still, the very thought of handing my gorgeous, defenceless, sweet-smelling bundle to anyone is so awful I can't think about it without the tears appearing.

2 March

Have a long chat with Dave about the situation. While he talks, I look frantically at the sleeping baby and imagine some nanny from hell smothering him in my absence just 'cos I need to get my fix of 'normal life'. Am overwhelmed and racked with guilt.

At this stage Dave says he thinks that even Mary Poppins herself wouldn't be good enough. Annoyingly, he's right.

We come to the conclusion that this is the perfect example of how both being self-employed should work to our advantage. David says he'll juggle things around so he can have Louis whilst I work, and thus, for the time being, we don't need to worry about childcare. Phew! I can now look forward to starting my new job.

5 March

New job on the horizon and feeling quite at one with the world, so we decide to have a family day out to St Andrews. Fresh air and a change of scene – yes please! The weather is lovely when we arrive and park at the side of the Old Course Hotel.

Dave gets the pram out of the car whilst I change into my walking boots for a good stomp through the town. As I get organised, Dave pushes Louis right up to the fence and starts talking to him about golf. As he points out some blokes coming up to the eighteenth green, he realises that the wee man can't see them so tilts the pram for him to have a better look. It suddenly dawns on me and I shout, 'Dave, have you . . .' But that's as far as I get as the answer to the remainder of the question, '. . . secured the pram to the base?' becomes apparent when the pram, complete with baby, flies off the wheelbase, flips right over and lands upside down on the ground.

'Louis!' we both screech and I run like hell over the car park to where Dave is lifting the upturned pram up, only to reveal a shocked-looking upside-down baby lying on the grass. As soon as he sees his eejit parents, he opens his mouth and lets rip. Now, in these circumstances, the main thing is to make sure that the baby is all right. To this end we independently move all his legs and arms around and feel overwhelming relief that he's still in full working order.

At this point I'm sure any agony aunt would suggest the no-blame approach and that one should take a deep breath and walk away rather than berate your partner. Yeh, right! The ranting, raving and jumping up and down is bad enough, but add to this the expletives and no wonder poor David looks more upset than Louis and just as upset as I am. The incredible bouncing baby. It's a quiet journey home.

6 March

Feel guilty about shouting at poor LSH yesterday. It could just as easily have been me. I decide to apologise for my unprecedented ranting and during the process think I'll make him feel better by telling him about the baby-rolling-off-the-bed incident. Dave's horrified that I didn't confess to this earlier so, rather than making things better, we're still huffing with each other as the sun goes down. But as we both sit with our arms folded and our legs tucked up under us, ignoring one another whilst watching a lot of crap on the TV, we catch each other's eyes and start laughing. It does seem ironic that we have a child upstairs asleep in his cot whilst downstairs we're behaving no better than a couple of ten-year-olds. Have a pillow fight and collapse, relieved that we've made up.

7 March

My old friend Holly is coming over for lunch. How we are friends, I'm not sure. She's a perfect physical specimen, a fitness queen who's practised aerobics for years. Just before her baby was conceived, in fact, she got so into it she actually became a teacher! I haven't seen her since she fell pregnant and can't help feeling guilty that I'm harbouring a desire that she'll be exhibiting some human characteristics and have gone to seed – complete with stretch marks and saggy tits.

Rats! I knew the second her toned leg slipped out the side of her Nissan Micra that my hopes were not to be realised. She looks bloody fantastic. Honed, toned, made-up, smiling, lively and with that spring in her step that only the truly addicted to exercise ever really achieve. I howk up my black leggings, put my fake and fixed grin on my face and open the door to her. There's no getting away from it, I have to tell her how wonderful she looks. If I don't, I'll be the only person in Europe who hasn't ooh-ed and aah-ed at her gorgeousness, thus instantly showing myself up as the jealous and bitter woman that I so obviously am. So, even before she gets her foot over the threshold, this compliment opens the floodgates as she beams back with a well-practised, 'Oh, not really, but thanks.' Then I get a day-by-day account – like I need reminding – that she did of course continue doing aerobics classes during the early stages of her pregnancy. In the later stages even she had to admit defeat in the leaping-up-and-down stakes so, not to be foiled completely, she then took up yoga for pregnancy. Ah, yes. I distantly recall buying a book with the same title, but what I did with it after that is a mystery. And it seems that virtually the day after her baby Josh was born, Holly – ignoring all medical advice – was back leaping around, limbering up and raring to go. Pah!

By this point in her monologue, I'm pinching myself to stay awake and when she eventually draws breath, I interject with a rather overenthusiastic, 'Right, then, shall we have lunch?' So we have lunch. Well, I do, starting with coronation chicken from M&S – creamy, yummy – which remains untouched by her fork. She chooses just to pick at the bag of salad which, as a tradition in our family, gets put out on the table in a large, colourful dish because it looks wonderful, but is then largely ignored. As she crunches through her leaves and I gorge on the mayonnaisey creaminess of the chicken, I make an internal promise to do fifty sit-ups a day. I mean, how hard can that be, for God's sake? I can do it first thing in the morning, or even watching telly at night. I also make the executive decision not to take out the profiteroles and ice cream and an hour or so later, once we've let the babies stare at each other and roll around together, she leaves. Phew! First thing I do is dive into the kitchen and get stuck into the profiteroles.

Once I've put cling film over the salad that Holly hasn't managed to get through, I go upstairs to put Louis down for his nap. Then I lie down in the room next door and do fifty sit-ups. Feel sick – primarily because my tummy is still full of chicken and profiteroles – but mentally I feel much better for it. If it makes any difference to the water balloon that inhabits the place where my stomach once was, then it'll be worth it.

8 March

7 a.m.

Wake up and can't move. Can't sit up. Think I'm having a late haemorrhage of some sort. Can't get out of bed.

I manage to roll over, but Dave has to winch me up whilst holding on to my hands. Using this humiliating method of elevation, he heaves me to my feet.

'What do you think's wrong with me?' I ask, expecting him to say, 'You're probably dying.' But his explanation is more feasible than that.

'It's the bloody sit-ups,' he says smirking. He did his best to try and hide his amusement last night as I lay moaning on the floor, demonstrating my new exercise regime, but now I realise this is more serious than I thought.

7 p.m.

Steer myself on to the floor. Will do more sit-ups.

7.01 p.m.

Have managed a paltry ten sit-ups and am now reclining on the carpet watching *Emmerdale* on TV. God, I don't even like *Emmerdale*, but even this is preferable to exercise. As I lie there it's difficult to concentrate on the screen with the large area of flesh that is my stomach spread in front of me, reminding me to get on with it. I watch my tummy intermittently during the ad break and then continue to alternate between *Emmerdale* and my tummy for the second half of the programme. Not sure which one is more entertaining. If I put on one of Holly's Lycra-style body-huggers, perhaps I could set myself up as a vaguely amusing Fringe act at the Edinburgh Festival. Why not just come along and have a bloody good laugh – no jokes, no plot, just a huge, wobbling fatty in a lurid, pink, shiny suit. I've paid money and seen worse.

9 March

Roll out of bed on to all fours. My guts are agony. Feel like I'm doing myself more harm than good. Think I need a grown-up to guide me in this quest for fitness, so make a few phone calls and then decide that the answer is to join a gym. At least it's a step in the right direction.

I drive down to see the place. It's vast and has lots of shiny, torturous-looking exercise machinery strewn around the place. I'm given a tour by Shawn, a tremendously thin and fit woman who makes me feel like Nellie the Elephant. I carry Louis in his car seat all the way and, by the time I've seen lots of other fit and firm women and men in Lycra, I want to run home and hide in a tent. I know damn well it's not going to get any better until I take control and I vow that soon, I too will be a fitness queen. With visions of Holly and her firm thighs in my flabby mind, I sign on the dotted line. I've taken the first step.

I go home and phone Jeffy. Give her my glad tidings about

being an official member of a gymnasium. She's suitably impressed and adds, 'Oh, I didn't know they had a crèche.'

Gulp. I say a hurried farewell and phone the gym. She's right,
they don't. Arrange to go in and get my money back. Fate is
conspiring against me and my stomach – plus I can't believe I
walked around the whole place with my baby in his car seat and
forgot to ask the question. Guilt over being a bad and evil
woman is back. Vow to find a gym with a crèche and some fat
members, then I think I might even go.

10 March

I remember people saying to me before Louis arrived, 'Oh, now
you take it easy. You'll need your rest and sleep. Sleep as much
as you can because once the baby arrives – ho, ho, ho! – it just
won't be the same after that.' Why didn't I listen? Pray tell me
what misplaced arrogance and ignorance made me think I'd be
any different. Now I wish I'd taken a year off just to sleep. The
thought of twelve hours of uninterrupted, deep, dreamless sleep
is as good as it gets. Just imagine. Swoon.

12 March

Today is the day for starting the wee pudding on solid food.
The idea is that it'll fill him up and make him a little less reliant
on me. With the radio show imminent, this is important, of
course – as is my need to get the hell out of the house, meet my
friends and have a life.

Have been preparing for this momentous occasion by, well,
buying baby rice and reading the back of tins a lot. Decide to
start him with the baby rice. I place Louis in his car seat on the
kitchen table, put a big bib on him and make up the mixture.
He watches me, looking bemused as I walk towards him talking
and brandishing a small, plastic spoon with gunge on it. The

wee sausage doesn't even realise I'm going to put it in his mouth, so I gently open it a little and slip the spoon with gunge inside. His eyes cross and he just sits there for a second, before the contents of the spoon come out twice as fast as they went in. I try again but have no luck. Having had a taste of baby rice myself, I can see his point. I wouldn't thank my mother for a blob of tasteless gunge either. It's official – baby rice is dull.

Four months old

13 March

Ask around a few friends and it seems that this is the way to start the eating regime. So despite my personal revulsion with the stuff, I try the baby rice thing again today and miraculously some of it stays in. Hallelujah!

Today I also find another gym – this time with a crèche. To the untrained eye and thigh it looks exactly the same as the last one. Basically, a torture chamber with fit people. Make an appointment to get a programme developed for me. Going along in a couple of days. Will have to find some sort of exercise sack to wear.

14 March

Start buying newspapers and magazines in preparation for my new show. I had no idea I was so out of touch with what has been going on in the world. I'm normally a voracious reader, but have picked up no reading matter whatsoever since Louis was born – other than the usual pamphlets and manuals on babies. It seems the world has been busy, and as I pore over some glossy women's mags, I do mourn the old me in jeans, striding down Princes Street with a smile on my face, a glint in my eye and a plan. Still, this is the first step to reclaiming some of that.

16: March

First things first. I spend an hour and a half in BHS trying to find some clothes to exercise in. Go for the comfy, black-sacks approach. Persevering, I try to buy a sports bra, but they don't come in the monstrous size my fun bags are at the moment.

I'm hot and sweaty and Louis is grizzling for a feed by the time I get to the gym. Gazing through the glass window at the crèche, I'm seriously tempted to put myself in with the babies for an hour. I'd be more than happy to lie on my back on a beanbag, order up some intravenous coffee and eat donuts. Have a good look at the girl who's in charge. She looks nice, gentle and sober. I even ask her if Louis so much as makes a squeak to come and find me. She nods in the 'another paranoid mother' way and off I go to have my fitness assessment done.

Firstly, I'm told to sit down and answer a series of questions. Then I'm weighed. Although I know I'm not exactly shedding my excess weight, it's still a terrible shock to hear the words 'thirteen-and-a-half stone' coming back at me. Stunned into depressed silence, I stand as she then straps on a heart-rate monitor, which I comment will be uncommonly high due to the shock of hearing how much I actually weigh. She ignores my attempt at humour as she guides me on to the exercise bike and tells me to pedal at my own pace for five minutes. Five minutes? Sounds like a moment – feels like an hour. Breathless, panting and sweating, I'm then given a glass of water and am rather hoping for a lie-down whilst she holds my hand and breaks the news as to how unfit I am. But no, there's no time for that sort of namby-pamby nonsense. No, no, no. She puts me straight on the running machine.

'You can watch telly whilst you're running,' she says as she wanders off with her clipboard and stop-watch. Scowling at her tortuous regime, I decide to walk briskly rather than run. Even at this pace all I can hear is my heart beating in my ears. I can't hear the telly, let alone see it through the rivulets of sweat pouring down my forehead and into my eyes. Tina – Ms Superfit – meanders over and encourages me to up the speed, so I break into a jog. Not only does my heart hit my ribs so hard I feel it might just burst, but more urgently, my chest begins to heave around, moving from side to side and up and down. It has a will of its own. There's no doubt in my mind that I need extra insurance because my chest is undoubtedly going to knock me out. It's heavy, sore and completely uncontrollable. I tell her to stop the machine and as it slows to a halt I gently cradle a boob in each hand, remove the heart monitor and limp back to the changing-rooms, ignoring her look of incredulity. Her time will come.

After I've retrieved Louis from the crèche, I return to reception and cancel my membership. This whole thing will have to wait till I'm fitter to get fit.

19 March

Louis has certainly got the hang of the baby-rice munching. Not only does he smile broadly when I announce it's lunchtime, but his legs kick wildly and his face goes red with excitement when he sees me brandishing the wee plastic spoon. It's just white sludge really. Hardly the most appealing thing I've ever seen. Surprisingly, though, he seems to be developing a taste for it – if you can 'develop a taste' for something with absolutely no taste at all.

Have been trying to stay awake later than 10 p.m. to read up on my topical newspapers for the imminent radio show. I can't. I'm in an information vacuum, but as soon as I get into a horizontal position, I fall asleep. So I'll just have to rely on the newspapers on the day, as even if I could read anything, I'd forget I'd ever seen it as soon as I put it down again!

20 March

Start the show tomorrow so head down to the radio station just to familiarise myself with the equipment again. All commercial radio is self-operated and so the way the show sounds is very much led by how competent the presenter is with all the technical wizardry – and that's before they even get a chance to open their mouths.

I'm somewhat traumatised to see that this is a state-of-the-art radio station and there's therefore no need to even touch a CD. It's all on hard disc and thus all you need to do is play with a mouse and stare at a screen. Blimey! Luckily someone has offered to sit in with me tomorrow in case I press delete and in one fell swoop wipe out the radio station altogether. In my current state of permanent tiredness and confusion, nothing's beyond the realms of possibility.

21 March

Up early and feed Louis as much as I can before drinking copious cups of coffee to wake my body and brain up. My show is on between 10 a.m. and 1 p.m. I arrive at the studio for 9 a.m. with all the newspapers under my arm and sit and have a good read. When I look up again, I still have fifteen minutes till my show starts. I'm determined not to phone home. I go to the loo, make another cup of coffee and still have ten minutes to go. I can't help myself. I phone Dave.

'You've only just left!' he says.

'I know, I know. Is Louis OK?'

I can tell LSH is expecting this and has all his stock answers to hand. And after the third or fourth idiotic question, he says, 'Alison, he's fine. Now bugger off and make some money!' So off I go into my airtight studio for three hours.

Surprisingly, it goes very well. If you don't include the moment when I'm in midflow and suddenly completely forget what on earth I'm talking about, that is. I have no idea. It's my topic, my rant and it goes completely out of my head mid-sentence. Eeek! I quickly shove on some music and pretend the three-second silence is a technical problem. Well, it's true in a way. It *is* a technical problem if my brain just shuts down.

I confess that during the ad breaks and news bulletins I phone home twice more. Judging by the answers I get from an increasingly exasperated Dave, it appears Louis can survive without his mother. How can he not be missing me? His mother, the woman who carried him for nine months. It seems I'm disposable. There's no more need for me.

22 March

Doing a Sunday show too. I promise Dave that I won't phone.

Before I know what's happening, halfway through the show during a news bulletin I pick up the phone and call. There's no reply. Why? Oh God, where are they? Oh no, I knew it! Something's very wrong. By the next news bulletin I've whipped myself into a frenzy with every worst-case scenario flitting through my deranged head. Dave has picked Louis up to carry him downstairs for lunch, tripped on the frayed bit of carpet at the top of the stairs, and they've both fallen down. Dave has broken his neck and Louis, injured, is lying in the crook of his dead father's arm bawling his eyes out.

Just as I'm about to put on a double album, phone the police and drive home, I look up and there, in the great big picture window that separates this studio from the office, is Dave with Louis in his arms. I put on a record and go out to see them – my boys. I get completely carried away and by the time I get back into the studio the lucky listeners have had 30 seconds of complete silence. Great start, Alison. Ban David and Louis from coming down again. Too distracting, but at least they're alive!

24 March

Although the radio show is only on two days a week, I'm trying – and failing – to keep up to date with the outside world now. I feel like I've been in a bubble of nappies, sick and lack of sleep for months and I'm finding it extremely hard to kick-start my brain. All I'm doing is telling jokes and playing records! I wonder how on earth those barristers and brain surgeons get up and go back to that level of intellectual challenge so soon after having babies? Mind you, I suppose they start off with a much bigger brain than my pitiful one in the first place. I started with a small- to medium-sized brain, which I'm convinced has diminished to chimp level by now.

25 March

No matter how many brightly coloured bits of plastic and fluffy toys Louis has around him, he's more interested in his own hands and feet. He lies on his back and plays with his toes and feet for hours. His new way of getting to sleep is to hold his hands up as if about to give a round of applause and then just watches intensely as he flicks his wee fat fingers gently against his other hand until he dozes off. Easily pleased.

26 March

My pal Elaine – her of nips-like-coat-hooks fame – comes round with a baby bouncer. It's a marvellous device which you suspend from a doorway – a long elastic cord under which the baby is held upright in a seat with a harness. This allows the child to bounce up and down like Skippy the Bush Kangaroo whilst you get on with whatever you have to. We attach the clamp above the doorway and put Louis into it. He'll get the hang of it soon – no pun intended! After half an hour he's still sitting still, looking confused with his legs dangling. Will try again tomorrow.

27 March

Terrible night last night. Investigate Louis's mouth. Could he be teething already? I don't know when they're supposed to produce their first tooth. Phone and ask Jeffy. It could be any time now. God, we had a few weeks of decent sleep once the baby rice kicked in and now they're just a distant memory. I've the radio programme tomorrow. I just hope I get a good night's sleep tonight.

28 March

Three hours' sleep max. Aaargh! Thank God it's radio. Hair on end, caffeine whirling round my system, I arrive to start the programme. Keep it together for the duration, but during the news bulletins at the top of the hour I have to go outside and stand in the fresh, icy cold Scottish air to snap me back into being really awake. Feel like I'm in a dream.

29 March

Even less sleep last night. No sign of teeth, but Louis is red-faced, grizzly and not happy. What on earth is going on? He's still eating his baby rice and suckling from me like a fiend. Manage to stay awake courtesy of my pal Fiona coming in and talking to me whilst the records are on. I just want to put my head on the desk and have a wee kip. She fills up my mug with coffee and feeds me Mars Bars and bananas instead.

30 March

Phone the health visitor. Louis's sleep has gone to pot and almost stopped. She suggests he might be hungry. I explain that he's sinking what feels like pints from my boobs and is wolfing into the baby rice. She insists it might be hunger and suggests

I start him on more solid foods. I tell her I'll try anything to get some rest. She suggests I stay in the spare room for a night and leave David with Louis.

'This is all very well, but what about when he needs feeding?' I ask.

'Have you tried him with a bottle?' she asks.

'Oh yes, and that was an unmitigated disaster.'

OK, solids it is.

31 March

Today I'm to introduce Louis to proper foods. No more baby rice, let's have some real, juicy, yummy grub. Have made the executive decision to make his mush myself. Well, it's only a few vegetables and a bit of fruit, for God's sake. This should give me even more freedom as his tummy will again reduce its reliance on my booberoos.

3.30 p.m.

God, it takes me ages to buy the vegetables, peel them and then boil them up. Then I spend ages mashing them in case a wee lump gets caught in his throat and he chokes and dies. As he sits on the kitchen table in his car seat looking bemused, he realises this is not the usual bland nonsense. Oh no, this is a new experience. The startling fun that is mashed carrot sits on his lips for three seconds before he does a rather impressive raspberry resulting in the lot spraying out again. He's having none of it.

I try courgettes next. Same result. Not amused. A cocktail of courgettes, apple and carrot? Baby rice and courgette? None of it's going in. None of it's being swallowed. I'm distraught. So it can't be hunger or surely he'd eat this stuff!

Dave arrives home. 'Oh my God, what's happened?' It isn't till I look up from my bib-and-spoon frenzy that I notice that all the kitchen surfaces and most of the pans, bowls, forks and plates are strewn over the kitchen. It looks as though I've cooked a dinner party for twelve, not just tried to feed one little baby. Who, incidentally, holds out for the baby rice, which I gratefully fill him with before sitting down and having a glass of wine.

2.45 a.m.

Breastfeeding Louis for the third time tonight. Can a child be fussy at this age? I wonder. Could I, the human dustbin, have given birth to a faddy eater? I try mixing carrot with courgette. Yes, I'm Nigella Lawson with smaller breasts, although Louis looks at me as if I'm Beelzebub when I feed him my latest concoction. I'm not resorting to tins. I'm a grown woman. I can boil vegetables up and make them appealing to a wee baby, for heaven's sake.

1 April

Mum appears.

'What's that?' I ask, as she produces a cheese wedge-shaped, metal grating device.

'It's a Mouli. It's for ricing food,' she explains and deftly rices some carrots and apple to demonstrate. Try Louis with it. Not on your life, his little pudgy face says as the food comes splurging out all over his chin and bib. Mullet is the only one who seems to be enjoying this process as the splats of various foodstuffs land on the kitchen floor and get slurped up by him. Amazingly, when I was down there today I found my *Yoga in Pregnancy* book. It was jammed under one of the legs of the kitchen table to stop it rocking about. A bit late for me to start that now, I suppose.

Try Louis with a bottle of formula and his lips snap shut. What am I to do? So exhausted I'm even afraid to drive the car in case I fall asleep at the wheel.

2 April

Friend Elaine comes round with her wee boy for lunch. As I forlornly Mouli up some veg, she produces a tin of boiled beef and carrots. It looks like shit and doesn't smell much better. As her wee boy wolfs it down, I persevere with today's delicacy of courgette and carrot – which is met with the usual reaction: disgust.

Before going forward to round two, I go to the loo. By the time I return not three minutes later Louis is wolfing down some boiled beef and carrots. Feel quite emotional. I've spent more time mashing and puréeing recently than is good for a sane person, only for my dedicated efforts to be endlessly rejected. The mere thought of the first thing to enter my baby's tummy – other than his mother's milk and some baby rice – being some revolting, bright-orange concoction from a tin that most likely consists of bulls' lips, eyeballs and God knows what else doesn't give me a happy glow. Bottom line is it's a monumental occasion and I missed it.

3 April

Now that Louis has finally grasped the fact that it's food that's on the spoon, he opens his mouth in anticipation – probably of some more boiled beef and carrot – I slip in some puréed carrot and apple and his mouth closes. His face contorts and grimaces, he swallows and his little moon-like face bursts into a gigantic, gummy smile. Success! Ta-da! Mullet is not amused, as it seems that stray splats of rejected food may be a thing of the past.

4 April
13 stone 6 pounds

Literally overnight, his sleeping dramatically improves. It must be all the boiled beef he's digesting – or not. It also means my sleep is marginally better.

Despite this, the determined little foot fiddler is still refusing any and all kinds of bottle. I've tried everything and have had no success whatsoever. Grrrrr! Until I can stop breastfeeding, I cannot see how I can seriously regain my pre-pregnancy shape. I read that breastfeeding naturally pulls the muscles of the stomach and uterus in. Bullshit – well, in my case. Even if this does happen internally, the fact that the baby is at me constantly gives me a humongous appetite – and when I say humongous, I mean it. I used to do a packet of Hobnobs at one sitting when suffering PMT from hell, but the way I'm feeling these days, a packet of biscuits would just be an appetiser. Basically, if it's not tied down, I'll eat it. No wonder Bone Dog is keeping out of my way. He knows he might be next.

10 April

Horrified. Today his grandma comes round to see him. He hasn't seen her for a few weeks and all he does is scream and cry and behave like she is, in fact, the devil incarnate. I'm mortified.

I ask Jeffy about it and she had exactly the same problem. Her son screamed blue murder when her sister came to the house when he was about this age. It seems they start to experience 'stranger danger'. Quite what kind of danger he is expecting from his gran we'll never know. Still, highly embarrassing.

11 April

Louis has a new trick. He can sit up without being supported. I'm very impressed with him but not as impressed as he is with himself. I sit him up and he sits there smiling like the Cheshire Cat.

When Dave comes in from work I tell him Louis has a new trick. I sit him up and he grins as he has done all day. David is so enthusiastic about his son sitting up unaided that he claps his hands and Louis bucks with joy – only to fly backwards and whack his head off the kitchen floor. He has a lump the size of an egg on his head, but is fine. Perhaps we should keep a cushion behind him after all.

Five months old

14 April

Every day since Elaine lent me the baby bouncer thing, I've put Louis in it for a few minutes to see if he gets the hang of it. Well, today he does. He masters the baby bouncer and is leaping up and down with his little rubbery legs, catapulting himself around the doorway. He loves it and whoops with joy as he pings from one side to the other. It looks hilarious and Bone Dog is terrified of him. It's remarkable how quickly it all happens. It was just a matter of weeks ago that we arrived home with a small, pink, immobile person who scared us half to death and here he is now, attached to a long piece of elastic, pinging himself around in our house and making a great deal of noise and mess along the way.

17 April

Dave thinks a night out together would perk us up. Who on earth can we get to look after Louis? David's sister Kirsty offers. This is great news, so we plan to go out.

I find a black stretchy item to detract from the body and over-apply the Yves Saint Laurent Touche Eclat that some kind soul has bought me. This is the highlighter stuff you put under your eyes to hide the bags. It has some job on its hands, but after a few layers of the stuff I think I do look almost human.

We're just going to go to the local Italian restaurant as, with

Louis still relying on my boobs, I can't even offer Kirsty a bottle to pacify him if he wakes up when we're out. On the way, Dave and I make a pact. We will not talk about Louis. Yeah, right. No sooner are we in the car than we're talking about how strange it is just to be out, the two of us together, without the baby. By the time Dave has parked the car, we're wondering if he'll be OK. The wee little thing, the product of our love, alone in our house without his parents. As my anxiety levels rise again, Dave reminds me that his sister is far better qualified to look after Louis than we are anyway. This is, of course, true and I know he'll be absolutely fine.

As we're perusing the menu, Dave just looks at me and knows exactly what I'm thinking. He rolls his eyes and tells me to phone Kirsty to check that everything's OK. I dig out my mobile and do just that. Of course he's fine. I'm being completely neurotic, I know that. I just can't help it.

'Shall we have a starter?'

'No, just a main course, I think.' There's no point in pretending I'm not hungry. We both know it's so that I can get home as quickly as possible.

We do manage to talk about other things for a few moments, but generally fail to stay off our pet subject so Louis and his day-to-day development dominate the evening. We're incredulous at how we could have thought the arrival of this little person wasn't going to change our lives. Everything has changed: where we live, how we live, what we want to do, where we want to go, what we talk about! Phew! It's completely overwhelming.

We get back before nine. Who'd have thought it? Kirsty smiles. She knows. We thank her profusely and as she says goodnight we both run upstairs to stare at our sleeping wee baby.

18 April

Uncle Sandy and Auntie Mary come to stay for a couple of days. He's bloody hilarious. An ex-rugby-playing opera singer, he's about seventy-five and the life and soul of the party. He used to think I was the life and soul of the party too – well, I was – and must be wondering who this white-faced, neurotic zombie is who now inhabits the place I once was.

Dave cooks dinner and I sit and listen to the conversation without taking much in. Halfway through the meal, tiredness floods over me and I've no choice other than to lay my head on the table. There is a break in the conversation and David nudges me.

'Do you want to go to bed?' he asks. I nod and shuffle off.

19 April
3 a.m.

Am woken by terrible crash. I sit up in bed. Dave sits up next to me. What the hell is that? He jumps up and puts his dressing-gown on. All I can hear is a deep groaning and moaning. Oh God, Uncle Sandy!

We rush downstairs. It seems Sandy got out of bed and lost his footing in the dark. To steady himself, he reached up and grabbed the curtains which, courtesy of a few elastic bands and a wing and a prayer, had been hung by me and would have fallen down if someone had so much as breathed hard on them. Poor Sandy. So rather than support him, they'd just given way under his not-insubstantial weight so that he now lay prostrate on the floor in agony.

'Shall I phone an ambulance?' I ask Auntie Mary – who is, incidentally, a doctor.

'For God's sake, Sandy, shut up and get into bed!' she shouts. 'You'll wake the whole bloody house.' With this, she turns over and goes back to sleep as Uncle Sandy is winched by David and me back into his bed.

9.30 a.m.

As we all sit around the table this morning – Louis in his high-chair, David in his suit, me in my dressing-gown – Auntie Mary emerges looking fresh as a daisy.

'How's Sandy?' I ask.

'Och, he'll be fine. He's just mithering about nothing,' she says.

10.45 a.m.

Uncle Sandy emerges, unable to walk or breathe properly. He's due to go to a rugby match, but instead has to sit propped up in the lounge as I feed him tea, sympathy and whisky.

By the time they're due to go home, he's in a wheelchair and has been diagnosed with two broken ribs and a bruised coccyx. After wheeling him over the tarmac at Edinburgh Airport, we wave farewell. At least he hasn't had a chance to notice what a zombie I've become as, by the time he leaves, we're a pretty sad matching set!

20 April

Despite Louis sleeping much better, I'm still a wreck. Decide I'll go to see the doctor as I'm not sure I'm coping. I've a lovely baby, a lovely husband, a dog that lives and a house with a toilet door! So why do I feel exhausted, anxious and out of control most of the time?

The doctor is brilliant and explains that there's a delicate balance of hormones in our brains and things like having a child can easily knock that balance off – which can result in our feeling like this.

'It happens to a lot of women,' he says, 'so don't worry, it's perfectly normal.'

A lot of women feel like this? Even hearing this makes me feel absolutely wonderful. So, as it turns out, I'm not mad! I'm not going to feel this utterly knackered for the rest of time. This is great news and cause for celebration. I tell him I just wish someone had told me honestly what it'd be like having a baby as opposed to just giving me a handful of primary-coloured pamphlets featuring lots of serene, smiling, clean and organised women in sky-blue nighties with waists and tiny babies. They make it look easy and natural and that's what I expected. And, well, it's just not like that at all.

23 April

It's amazing how much better I feel after talking to the doctor. Just knowing I'm not the only person in the known universe who frets and sweats and worries about being a good enough mother. The overwhelming guilt I feel when I want to shout and cry and walk away is OK too, and the need to go out and work and be Alison, the individual, as well as Alison, Louis's mum, apparently does not make me an evil, hateful bitch either. Yahoo! Someone should do a pamphlet with *that* sort of information in it – with a photograph of a knackered, overweight woman in a baggy maternity dress and with red nipples, vomit on her shoulder and a small baby. That would be a pamphlet worth bloody reading. In fact, I could model for it and gladly would.

30 April

Louis is taking this eating thing to extremes now. He'll eat anything and everything. I found him with the front door Yale key in his mouth this morning. I was almost sick with panic when I turned round and saw him determinedly chewing down on something. I asked him to open his mouth but he refused point blank so I prised his mouth open with my fingers and rescued the key as it slipped around on his tongue. I reattached it to a key ring pronto. He's also making some real inroads into rolling and rocking and I don't think it'll be long till he's actually moving around under his own steam. This'll open up another huge realm of possibilities when it comes to potential face-stuffing and danger.

1 May

Meeting pals in Glasgow for lunch. Now, this is a big outing on the train for the three of us. They're a child-free couple, so we're determined to be in control and not smelling of baby puke and looking like a bag of washing.

We start early and arrive at the restaurant in good time. We get a high-chair for Louis, who is sitting – clean and smiley – as our pals arrive. We order drinks and are looking at the menu when my friend Elaine gestures at Louis.

'Is he all right?' she asks and I turn and see his face going red. Not just flushed pink, but a colour that deepens until it's a dark, red-purple. 'Is he choking?' she adds.

'No, I think he's having a . . .' It's at this precise moment that a loud, staccato rumble begins to emanate from his bottom. And he continues to bring us this charming noise as his face eventually returns to its normal colour and with it a big smile.

Griff and Elaine can't believe that such a comedy farting noise has emanated from this smiling wee baby as I laugh, man-handle him out of the high-chair and make my way to the ladies'. Here there are no proper changing facilities – not even an area that's big enough to lie him down – and as I stand, wondering what to do next, I feel it. A wet sensation on my hand. A quick look in the mirror shows the reflection of Louis's back. Basically, the shit has hit everything it possibly can without actually hitting the fan. As I stand helplessly wondering what to do next, it begins to run from the inside of his trousers and drip from his feet on to the floor of the loo. My heart beats wildly.

We're in a restaurant. We're with people who don't have children. We have no change of clothes with us. We have left the car in Edinburgh.

I put my best fixed grin in place, take my jacket off to wrap casually round the baby and wander back to the table, saying to Dave, 'Can I have a word, please?'

He follows me round the corner till we're out of sight and I wheeze at him, 'He's done a gigantic jobbie and it's absolutely everywhere. You'll have to go and buy him something to wear.'

Dear Dave. Not missing a beat, he goes back to the table, drains his glass of wine and casually says, 'Back in a few minutes,' before turning and sprinting out the door. I retreat back into the ladies to wait, smiling at women as they come in and recoil at the God-awful smell which is permeating the air.

Fifteen minutes later there's a knock at the door and it's Dave with some new clothes.

'For God's sake, come in!' I say as we wrestle Louis's sodden clothes off him and hold him squirming over the basin till he's clean. We dry him under the hand drier – which upsets him no end – and then dress him again before sashaying out of the ladies' and back to the table to eat our by now very cold food. Not what I would deem a raging success really. Don't think Griff and Elaine will be rushing off to procreate.

3 May

Louis's six-month check with the health visitor. We go and sit in the waiting-room for ages till it's our turn. When we're shown into her office, he's measured and weighed before she asks me a few questions about his development. Then she sits him on my knee and walks up behind us to clap her hands and test his hearing. He completely ignores her. Well, you would if you were living in a house where there's the constant noise of dog, human, phone, TV, music, piano, computer, doorbell and so on. She does her stealthy hand-clapping a second time and then sits down opposite me and looks very serious. She tells me two things. Firstly, that he has a squint and secondly that he's deaf. I feel tears welling up in my eyes. I want to protest that there's nothing wrong with my perfect baby, but she's the grown-up so I listen and leave feeling deflated and upset.

When I get home I phone my sister-in-law and tell her what the health visitor has said.

'Oh, they said exactly the same about Amy.'

'They didn't!'

'They bloody did.'

I'm so relieved. My instincts tell me he doesn't have a squint and a deaf ear, but if I were younger and more easily led I'd be in bits right now. Make a mental note to get the woman back.

5 May

Buy a copy of *Hello!* magazine and wish I hadn't bothered. Every new mum in here has lost about three stone in a week. They go on holiday to hot places with small babies and wear bikinis! It's obscene. How can this be? I haven't worn a bikini for five years. We booked a holiday today. It's not until September and this must be my goal. To be back in fighting-fit shape by then. Whatever that is.

6 May

David and I have decided not to get straight-eyed, clear-eared Louis christened in a religious ceremony. I wasn't christened and although there are those who think I'll die and go to Hell, personally I'll wait till I'm ninety-three with a terminal illness before I jump on any particular religious bandwagon. I did dabble with becoming a Mormon when I was in love with Donny Osmond, aged thirteen, but soon found out that they can't drink alcohol and give ten per cent of their income to the Church. So that was that. But hey, that's just me. David, on the other hand, was christened but is not a regular church-goer so together we feel it'd be hypocritical to go down that route. When Louis grows up he can decide for himself if he wants to follow any particular faith. Still, we don't want to forego the opportunity of having an excuse for a party, so we opt for a combined head-wetting and house-warming. We decide on 23 May.

Six months old

22 May

Off to buy the drinks for the party tomorrow. It's funny. I used to look askance at women in supermarkets who talked loudly to their children and sang. Why? Of course you speak to them. They're human beings. Well now, as they say, the boot is on the other foot. I'm not averse to swanning round Sainsbury's singing 'The Wheels on the Bus' or making a selection of idiotic faces to keep the wee sausage amused. I now appreciate the scowling faces of the uninitiated looking at me with pity – as if I'd be better served showing the baby flashcards and talking to him about economics in French.

23 May

We have a bouncy castle. I won't stand too close to it in case, in the half-light and half-cut, people try to jump on to me – there's a worrying resemblance. Dave's restaurant does the outside catering so we have a long trestle-table groaning with food and, of course, the kitchen is completely cleared out for drinks.

Unbelievably, it's a sunny day, and people start to arrive. Louis is on great form and spends the majority of the afternoon smiling at people and being perfect.

6 p.m.

Most people with small kids have left and I'm trapped here with a house full of adults, several of whom – as predicted – have had far too much to drink and are on the bouncy castle. They seem to be in their second childhood.

At this juncture Louis starts grizzling. It's only to be expected but I cannot get him to be quiet and I'm exhausted. As I stand here wondering what to do next, Auntie Margaret comes up and reads the situation perfectly. She produces a bar of Cadbury's Dairy Milk from her handbag, unwraps it and puts the end into Louis's open mouth. He's silenced instantly. His mouth clamps down over the bar and, for the first time I've ever seen, he smiles broadly whilst sucking madly. It's a hit.

24 May

5 a.m.

Up with Louis. The entire house is strewn with bottles, plates and ashtrays. I've neither the energy nor the urge to clean it up.

7 a.m.

Have already fed Louis, got dressed and feel like lunch. I get an overwhelming urge for a big cooked Sainsbury's breakfast and an hour later I'm standing outside the supermarket waiting for it to open.

Before Louis, there's no way I'd ever have imagined myself standing impatiently outside Sainsbury's waiting for it to open. And the most amazing thing is, I'm not alone. This secret world must have existed for as long as babies have been born and supermarkets have been invented.

As I stand here I see a few other bleary-eyed souls. One of them is a guy I do voice-overs for. He's head of a big ad agency in town and I've never before seen him in anything other than a sharp suit looking slick, smart and efficient. Well, here he is, hair on end, bloodshot-eyed, in a baggy, stained tracksuit with his rug rat in a pram and looking bloody miserable.

'Hello!' I say.

He squints at me. 'Oh, hello,' he replies. We don't need to say another word. We just shrug our shoulders as if to say, 'How the heck did this happen?'

When the door to the supermarket opens, we smile at one another. We're not alone.

25 May
13 stone 5 pounds

OK, so the gym thing hasn't happened but *something* has to. Nothing much is changing in the body-shape department and now it's hot summer and I'm wearing long, baggy jackets to cover my long, baggy trousers. I've spoken to Jeffy, who told me she used to put Lyle in the pram and just walk round Edinburgh. It's a good way to get out of the house, get some fresh air and get fit. Sounds perfect – especially for an Aberdonian, as it's also free!

Make a start today. After breakfast I get Louis into his pram and we go walk-about. I take Bone Dog along as well and we cover quite a few miles. We stop at the supermarket on the way back to get a few bits and pieces, but of course Mullet isn't allowed inside. I tie his lead to a post and Louis and I go round. I fill the trolley with messages and as we're at the check-out I'm interested to see that Louis is now shopping too. I hadn't noticed that he'd been grabbing items and putting them in the trolley too. Although clearly he can't read, it seems he already has an eye for expensive chocolate. Reluctantly, I put it back. There's little point in stomping the streets if I gorge myself on choccies.

Pleased with my new regime, we emerge from the supermarket to retrieve Bone Dog. I can't believe my eyes. He's gone. Gone! My beloved mongrel, stray, unloved, unwanted Irish hound has disappeared. His lead is here, his collar is here but the Bone is gone. I don't know what to do. I haven't got my mobile with me so I run back to the house, pushing the pram uphill until I'm wheezing and sweating profusely.

Arriving home I phone Dave and explain what's happened. 'Someone's stolen him!' I announce dramatically.

'Don't panic,' says Dave. 'I'll phone the police and the cat and dog home. You get into the car, drive about and see if you can find him.'

I change Louis quickly, put him into the car seat and drive around the streets looking for our lovely dog. After an hour there's still no sign of him but, as I turn round to head home, I see a woman of about my age, with similar long, dark hair, pushing a pram. I get nearer to her and I see there's something by her side. As I pull up, I notice it's a collie. I stop the car, jump out and walk round.

'Excuse me' – she jumps a little – 'is that your dog?' At this point the fool dog turns round and looks at me. It's Bone Dog! He looks at this woman – with the same hair, the same style of jacket, a pram – and then looks at me. His daft face looks confused. The silly bloody mutt has been following this poor woman all the way from the supermarket thinking it's me!

'He's a lovely dog,' she says.

'Yes, but the lights are on and nobody's even popped in,' I explain as I laughingly open the back of the car and he slopes in, looking as if even he is feeling a little ridiculous!

26 May

Do the walking thing but today leave Bone Dog at home. Put a photograph of me and Louis by his basket and tell him to memorise it by the time we get back.

28 May

As we stomp the streets of Edinburgh, I get a new perspective on the city. It really is a beautiful place. I've never really opened my eyes to it before, having driven around it since I first arrived. But now I'm very excited that I'm lucky enough to live in such an amazing place and I chit-chat to Louis about it as we wend our way through the streets and into town.

Much to my delight, Louis has started to gibber back at me. He makes the sounds and oohs and aahs of real talking, only I don't understand a word of it. He's a babbler. It must be hereditary.

9 June

Having a lovely summer. We spend a lot of time outdoors. I let Louis rumble about the grass and try not to look too concerned as he shovels mud and grass into his mouth. It didn't do me any harm, I try to remember. However, when I turn around this afternoon and see only half a worm hanging from his mouth, I do react a little more instantly – snatching it out whilst opening his mouth up with my other hand to see if the other half is still in there. God, I hope he hasn't swallowed it.

Worry all day for no reason, it seems. He's as fit as a fiddle and eats a massive tea – so it seems that Milky Ways aren't the only things you can have between meals that won't spoil your appetite!

Seven months old

19 June

Dave comes home with some exciting news. He's just bought an old bank building, which will be turned into a restaurant in the Bruntsfield area of Edinburgh. There's another one on the way!

He arrives with five people from work. It's a beautiful day and we all sit out in the garden celebrating.

20 June

Louis and I are up early, clear headed and ready for action. Due round to Jeffy's for coffee. Dave's running late and asks if he can drop us off en route.

'Great idea,' I say as I gather my stuff together. 'Put Louis in the car and I'll be out in a sec.'

Well, it only takes a sec. Dave plops Louis into the car seat and into the car and then comes inside to grab his briefcase. By the time he gets back outside again, Louis has inadvertently pushed down the central-locking nodule in the back and is now firmly ensconced in the car on his own. Oh, how I laugh – until I see Dave's face.

'The car keys are in the ignition.'

'What about the spares?' I ask, resisting the urge to kick him hard.

'In the glove compartment,' he answers in a voice that's barely audible.

Smiling so as not to panic Louis – who is also smiling and waving from the back seat – I say through clenched teeth, 'Well, you'd better phone the bloody police then. NOW!'

Dave runs into the house as I stand smiling and waving as calmly as I can at my trapped baby. It's a hot day and probably about seventy degrees in there. The windows are all closed tight and, given the amount of rubbish lying all over the back seat, I have no doubt he'll be stuffing it into his mouth. I'm beginning to experience blind panic.

Meanwhile, Dave phones the police and explains the situation. They say they'll be there asap. By now, Louis is starting to get upset. Waving and heating up inside a messy old car whilst your eejit parents pull faces and wave back from outside while refusing to open the door and get you out, feed you or comfort you has dawned on him as not really on.

By the time the polis arrive, Louis's hysterical, I'm hysterical and Dave's trying not to be hysterical. The polis quickly and efficiently take out the back window and one of them quickly scrambles in to release the central-locking system. We're so grateful we thank them profusely. They assure us it's no problem before rushing off to their next emergency call. At least that's what they say, but I suspect they realise there's going to be a real humdinger of a domestic unfolding the moment they're out of earshot. They're right.

21 June

Dave comes home with a baby-walker. Fantastic device – I've photos of me in one in the '60s. It has five sets of castors on it and the baby sits in a chair which is suspended over the base. Then, by using their feet, they can propel themselves across the floor.

We put Louis into it. He sits still for ages. I give it a gentle push to show him how it'll move if he pushes it with his feet. Still static.

By the end of the afternoon he's whirling around the kitchen and smashing into the units. It's Eddie Irvine in a baby-walker. Find the whole thing very funny indeed. He's thrilled.

23 June

Article in a magazine says baby-walkers can give your child bandy legs and discourage them from walking. Och. As we discuss this and I tell him it didn't do me any harm, Dave takes a step back and makes some very rude comment about my legs and that maybe we should get him out of it immediately. I remind him that our side of the family may well have short legs, but at least we have short torsos to match, whereas he's not only blessed with the shortest legs in history, but, by way of God's idea of a joke, he also has the longest back as well, giving him the appearance of being just that little bit further back down the evolutionary scale. One look at Eddie – who's stopped his whirling temporarily as his imbecile parents laugh and pull each other's very short legs – and we take the executive decision to leave him with it. He loves it. He is Mobile Man, and surely they wouldn't manufacture them if they were bad for kids, would they?

24 June

Decide to head off to the West Coast at the weekend. It's Dave's birthday soon and it'll be lovely to get away for a few days.

26 June

Head north. We're more used to travelling with the wee man now so it doesn't take quite so long to pack the car and get ourselves organised. Invariably, there's at least one crisis before we get to our chosen destination, but today everything runs smoothly. Dave's driving, Louis's in the back, Bone Dog's in the boot and the spare key for the car is in my handbag.

We check into the Dundonnell Hotel and put up the travel cot. We've even taken the baby-walker with us. Anything to try and exhaust Louis and get ourselves a good night's sleep. But we must have looked barking with all this paraphernalia as we pulled up outside, although the receptionist still smiled and welcomed us warmly.

27 June

It's David's birthday tomorrow. I ask him what he'd like and the answer is to go off fishing for a whole day and a night. What can I say? 'Rather you than me' is on the tip of my tongue, but I realise he means it and so I drive him to the bottom of a mountain and drop him off with his tent, his rod, his rucksack and a great big cheesy grin. I sit and watch as he walks off into the mountains until he's just a little dot on the horizon. I'm to pick him up at midday tomorrow in the same place. I don't know how he can do it. It'd be my idea of Hell, alone on a mountain for a night. Aaargh!

By the time he's out of sight, it dawns on me that here I am, left in the wilds of Gairloch with my wee pudding – who may just have realised he's left with his imbecile mother as he starts crying. I slide over to the driver's seat and start the engine, hoping this'll soothe him, but it seems not.

By the time we get back to the hotel – a fifteen-minute drive – he's still wailing. Nae, screeching. He's hot and bothered and will not be comforted. I pop him into the pram and we go for one of our walks. I chat to him about the trees and beautiful hills, but he can't hear me as he's still bawling! I really am at a loss as to what to do. After we've walked for a good hour, there's no let-up so I put him back in the car and drive around looking mad for a bit. Eventually I head back to the hotel, by which point I'm starving. Louis won't eat so I just sit on the bed, staring at the telly with the sound down hoping he'll eventually fall asleep.

I can't tell you how much I wish Dave was here. He could theorise as to what might be wrong, help to decide whether to call the doctor or not and generally keep things a bit calmer. But he's not, so I slop some Calpol into the wee man, put him back into the pram and walk – and walk and walk and walk until eventually, after two hours, he drops off.

By the time I walk back to the hotel I'm exhausted. I prise the sleeping Louis out of his pram, tiptoe into our room and successfully put him into his cot without waking him, before having a wee lie down on the bed to get forty winks.

11 p.m.

I wake up and a quick look at the clock tells me I've missed dinner. Bugger it. I'm absolutely starving. I scoff a tin of chocolate pudding and just as I finish it Louis awakes. He's been asleep for hours and is in tip-top form – laughing, smiling, dribbling and full of the joys. I dig out the baby-walker, put him in and he careers around the room, crashing into the walls and bed.

28 June

2 a.m.

Louis's the life and soul of the party.

4 a.m.

I feed him and he finally falls into a deep, milk-induced sleep. Phew!

6.15 a.m.

Wake up to the wee man crying again. Panicking now. Stuck in the middle of the Highlands with what I detect to be a sick child. Unable to get hold of LSH if I need to and worry that Louis really is ill. Try to remain calm and keep him quiet, but he's having none of it. Get him dressed, although he seems to prefer lying on his back with his legs stretched out straight as a board to being a malleable wee baby.

Eventually get him into some clothes and carry him downstairs for breakfast. He calms down as I put him in a high-chair and mash up some Weetabix. He looks quite interested in it as I raise the spoon and do the 'here comes the train' routine. His mouth flies open, I smile – everything's going to be fine – and then put the spoon in. He screams his head off, his face goes crimson and he's beside himself. He's making such a noise that even the most tolerant breakfast participant can't be expected to put up with it. Harassed, I scoop him up with a false 'you know kids!' face on, steer him out of the diningroom and go back to the bedroom.

He's inconsolable. And 5 ml of Calpol later he's still roaring so I decide on the car tactic. I bung him in his car seat and just drive up and down the same piece of road – a lot. If I don't, I'm afraid I'll get lost, and if I get lost, I won't be able to find where I am to pick David up again. If I miss picking David up, I'll be in deep despair.

Eventually Louis drops off, but I keep driving for fear that, if I stop, he'll wake up again. Open the windows to keep myself from dropping off – punch drunk in charge of a vehicle.

11.55 a.m.

I pull up at the designated spot and here he is – weather-beaten, filthy and with a huge grin on his face. David. Thank God.

As I turn the engine off to help him get his stuff into the boot, he asks, 'How are you?' And before I can answer, the blood-curdling scream begins again. I roll my eyes and get in the back. Dave's going to drive.

The noise is unbelievable as we travel along the road. 'Oh, happy birthday!' I shout above the din, at which exact point Louis stops wailing and gives me a huge, big smile – only to reveal . . . a tooth! A tiny, wee flash of white enamel in the middle of his bottom gum. Officially his first tooth and what a day to produce it too. All wailing and red-faced mitherings are forgiven – and that's just me – it's a milestone day. We buy him a chocolate pudding to celebrate, which he gamely smears all over his head, clothes and me, but he's a happy baby again. Thank you, God.

29 June

The reality of the tooth thing has suddenly hit home. Or should I say *bit* home. The wee fiend is now biting my boob. I can't get him to take a bottle – *I'm* on the bottle – but he's totally disinterested. This has to stop. I'm now being eaten alive.

30 June
13 stone 2 pounds

Back home in Edinburgh and on a mission to get Louis to take a bottle. He's resisted all attempts so far, but the arrival of the tooth has given the whole situation a sense of urgency. Off I go to Boots, where I buy various models, shapes and devices. Then I wait.

When Sir Suckalot is looking for milk, I gently warm bottle model no. 1 and hand it over to him. He puts it in his mouth, I smile, he then clamps his gums firmly together, shutting it out of his mouth and stays like that, fixing me with his big brown eyes as if to say, 'Come on, woman, you don't think I'm falling for that one, do you?' Not wanting to make a big issue of it, I don't persevere. It'll happen over the next day or two, it has to.

1 July
7.30 a.m.

Try bottle model no. 2. Still no luck. Boobs out again.

12.30 p.m.

Try bottle model no. 3. He sucks a little. Must have sensed a great wave of euphoria in me as he did so. Not having seen a lot of euphoria before in his baggy, red-nippled mother, he doesn't recognise it necessarily as a good thing so, with eyes on me at all times, spits this one out too.

I call my friend Kim for a bit of light relief and tell her that I'm giving up breastfeeding as seven months is too long. She's a teacher and she tells me that, at one of the schools she's taught at, every break time there was a woman who used to turn up at the perimeter railings, shout the name of her child and then, as he ran over, get her boob out and feed him through the railings. He was five.

2 July
1.30 a.m.

Dream I'm back in Aberdeen. Walking through the university campus, I approach the Red Lounge – a favourite hangout in the old days. I briefly scrutinise the subsidised lager prices and smile, before turning and seeing a group of familiar faces. Walking over to them, I say, 'Louis!' A boy of about eighteen looks up and I smile and begin unbuttoning my shirt.

Horrified, I wake up in a cold sweat. I was going to breastfeed an eighteen-year-old boy. Aaargh! Drastic action has to be taken. Now. I need my body back.

3 July

The bottle battle goes on, now made all the harder by the fact that Louis is beginning to move independently. He sits on all fours and sort of rocks back and forward with a very determined look in his eye. He'll be on the move soon and will be able to escape me as I chase him round the house with bottles various.

4 July

'It's Independence Day,' announces Dave. 'You're going out.'
  'What?'
  'Yes, you're going out to enjoy yourself and you'll come back to find Louis asleep and me in a calm and in-control state.'
  By the time he's finished the last sentence, I'm in my glad rags – black, voluminous – and feeling fretful. 'Are you sure you can cope? What'll happen if he doesn't take it?'

Twenty questions and twenty reasonable answers later, I'm in the car and speeding away from my husband, son and home. I feel light, happy . . . and terribly, terribly guilty.

I go to the cinema with my mates and can't concentrate on the film. We go out for supper afterwards and have a great laugh – a great tears-down-the-face, knicker-wetting, girlie night out.

11 p.m.

When I tiptoe in all is quiet. I go into the kitchen to see Bone Dog and give him a biscuit. On the kitchen table stands nothing but an empty baby's bottle and a piece of paper which simply reads, 'SUCCESS!' I could weep with joy, but have learned by now there's no point in weeping when you can sleep.

5 July

Wake up with super-sore boobs. It seems I'll have to wean myself off him! Slowly but surely. And then I'll have my body back.

While I phone my mum to tell her Louis has finally taken a bottle, his rocking back and forth moves on a step further and he crawls. He moves his fat, nappied bottom and he shuffles along the carpet. His face is a picture. He can't believe it. One minute he's at one end of the living room and the next, through the miracle of movement, he's at the other, twanging the phone cord as I speak to Mum. I pick him up, whirl him round and put him down again. He's delighted and spends the afternoon crawling one way, stopping, looking at me for a round of applause – which he duly gets – before crawling back again. Independence Day for him too.

When Dave comes home, he's thrilled when Louis meets him at the door smiling. He's lifted up and whirled around for the tenth time that day. As we sit down to catch up on the day's news, Louis continues to crawl about, at which point I hear the words, 'Don't put your fingers in there,' and Dave throws himself across the floor, picking the wee man up like a rugby ball, and lands on his side. Ah yes, the sockets.

Just as well he's finally on bottles. He needs more food now that he's belting round the house on all fours.

6 July

Another bloody secret is out. Once these wee guys start moving, life is over. They motor round the house looking for things to poke their tiny, pink and usually wet fingers into. Sockets, dogs' eyes, the fire, the video, the telly – I've not been on the floor for years and, when I get down there to have a look, I'm quite overcome with the number of dangers that lurk below.

Back to Mothercare for a selection of plug guards and cup-board-closing things. Dave's not a Handy Andy so we have to wait till my cousin's husband Mark comes to fit them all. He can't be here for a couple of days. No problem.

7 July

Problem! Problem! Cooking tea, he's behind me on the floor. I move him away. He's like a human boomerang, springing back. Mullet, the Bone Dog, looks terrified. Suddenly this noisy wee person is moving around and is fairly keen on having a good look at him. Mullet, whose eyes show terror, lies still and sort of clenches up as Louis crawls all over him. He's been in Mullet's basket today and when I take my eyes off him for an instant, he's had a taste of Pedigree Chum. Actually, he quite enjoyed it, which is good because the way my childcare arrangements aren't going, I'll never be able to work more than two days a week and we may all end up eating dog food before long.

The effect of all this exercise is a joy. Louis slept for twelve

hours last night. Yes, count 'em. *Twelve hours straight through!*
Of course, I didn't. I awoke every two hours 'cos that's what my
body clock now tells me to do. I got up a couple of times and
stood watching him sleep.

8 July
7 a.m.

I'm convinced Louis is in some sort of coma brought on by
formula milk. But no, he awakes like a wee angel, smiling and
stretching. I think we've turned a corner.

9 July

He slept thirteen hours last night. Jesu, joy of man's desiring.
This is great. I'm considering taking him to one end of the local
park and getting him to crawl the full length of it before bedtime.

6.30 p.m.

At teatime the phone goes. It's a walk-about phone and I leave
it everywhere, except recharging on its cradle. Running around,
I eventually find it under a pile of clothes in the lounge. As I
walk about talking to Jeffy, I look around for Louis, who is
suddenly nowhere to be seen. It's then I hear a familiar 'Goo!'
noise and look up. There he is at the top of the stairs, teetering
on the very top step and clearly delighted with himself for
having mastered another tricky move in life. And here I am at
the bottom with my heart in my mouth.

'What a clever boy!' I say in my most calm and reassuring
voice as I drop the phone, leap up the stairs four at a time and
grab him as he falls backwards like a stone into my arms. I
phone Mark and beg. 'Can you come today, please?'

10 July

Fort Knox. Every plug has a cover. The stair gates are at both top and bottom. The video is already broken thanks to a slice of toast that miraculously found its way in there, but we got a cover for this too so put it on anyway. The cupboards in the kitchen all have these catches on them now to prevent kids going in and drinking Ajax. The problem is, I can't work the darn things and keep shutting my fingers in them. Still . . . we're now prepared and ready for the mobile baby stage.

11 July
12 stone 8 pounds

Determined to do my sit-ups this morning. Am only five in when Louis decides to climb on top of me, jamming his fingers up my nose. It seems that this is his way of saying hello. Not pleasant and, depending on his trajectory, quite sore. I remove them immediately and say, 'No!' – which, of course, is baby language for, 'Do it again, please, now.' Still, it saves on hankies.

Eight months old

15 July

As he lies here having his last feed ever, with his fingers up my nose and dozing off, I feel very emotional. This is the end of the intense, intimate bond of breastfeeding.

As I consider it, tears well up in my eyes until a couple of them splash off my face and on to his. Suddenly his eyes roll back and open for a second. He looks at me with a glazed expression, says, 'Dada,' and then drops off again. What did he say? Dada! He spoke. The boy speaks. Dada.

Give this monumental news to Dada and try to hide the fact that I'd have been far more thrilled, given the context of the whole moment, if he'd decided to utter the name of the woman who gave birth to him, nurtured him and breastfed him until ten seconds ago – i.e. Mama. Decide to start training routine in the morning.

16 July
7.30 a.m.

Hear him rumbling around in his cot so go through and lift him up.

'Good morning, Louis. Mama, Mama, Mama, Mama.'

He looks at me and smiles. 'Dada,' he says.

Mmmm. This is going to take time.

19 July

We're off to a Russell and Amanada's wedding in London. My parents are having Louis for a couple of nights. It's the first time we've left him and I give them an instruction manual about sixty pages long. David looks at me and reminds me that they did bring me up. Yes, fair point. Ditch the sixty-page manual and go for one A4 sheet, mainly instructing them to say 'Mama, Mama, Mama' a lot in my absence. I can't help it.

We fly to London and meet up with Griff and Elaine for lunch. We're twenty-one again. We're free. We're rampaging. We eat and drink far too much.

After our four-hour lunch, we're wandering along a leafy lane on the way to the wedding venue where we're all staying when a long black car pulls up alongside us. The darkened, electric window slides down and a voice says, 'Come on, you lot, get into the car before I run you over.' It's my old pal, Andy, who's just arrived back from Dubai for the wedding. We're delighted to be: a) picked up; and b) in such a posh car.

As soon as we get to the hotel, we order up some more drinks

– which we continue doing until . . . well . . . the rest is frankly a mystery.

20 July
6.30 a.m.

Wake up wishing I'd been smothered with a pillow. I can't feel like this on the day of my best pal's wedding. It's not right. One look at the pale face next to me confirms that Dave too is in deep sufferance. We look at each other, roll our eyes and drink copious quantities of water. No sooner is our small pudding off with his grandparents for the weekend and we revert to type A: irresponsible adults trapped in the mindset of people altogether much younger and physically fitter.

We shake and fumble around, get dressed and go down for breakfast. We hear there's been a lot of unhappy guests due to a noise that went on all last night. We look at each other, hoping it wasn't us singing or me playing the piano. When I've had a few, I play the piano if there is one. I think I sound like Elton John, but I've been informed that it's really more Les Dawson.

Once he has an innocent enough expression on his face, Dave plucks up the courage to ask the waitress, 'What was the noise all about last night?'

'It's the peacocks rutting,' she replies – at which point seventy-five per cent of the guests in the breakfast room end themselves. You see, the surname of the best man and his wife – who're sitting on their own, also shaking violently having had a skinful last night – is Peacock.

After people have regained control of themselves, we all go outside and, amidst much hilarity, take photos of the human Peacocks standing beside the resident feathered ones.

11 a.m.

I must have still been drunk at breakfast. I can't stand up, I'm sweating and my high heels seem to be giving me vertigo. The hat I've brought is too tight, the thought of alcohol is repellent and the weather is so hot it'll probably be the death of me. Off we go, though – head up, buttocks clenched – to the wedding.

Beautiful ceremony and a glorious setting overlooking the River Thames in which to stand and sip champagne – if you can face the champagne. I know it'll end badly, so I stay on water for hours and hours till eventually I take the plunge. The plunge goes well and the next thing I know I'm on the stage singing 'Mustang Sally'.

21 July

Flying home today. Don't want to get on a plane feeling like this. I'm so dehydrated I may combust when we get up there. Desperate to see Louis, I go quietly. What will my parents think? We've been out of Scotland for less than forty-eight hours and look about fifteen years older. Louis will be gloriously ignorant of our bad behaviour, but we know we're still twelve at heart and probably not fit to be in charge of such an innocent wee bundle as our lad at home. Guilt. Guilt. Guilt.

Get home. Mum takes one look at me and she knows.

'Good wedding?' she asks, with a knowing smile. When I answer in a voice that's four octaves lower than usual, she tells me to sit down whilst she makes a cup of hot, sweet tea. Yes, she's lived with my father long enough to know the score.

23 July

Now that my breasts are mine again, they look a bit pissed off. I'm convinced they've shrunk. Shrunk and deflated to a sad state of affairs. They used to be quite perky in their own way, but that's all in the past. Looking down at them, I feel angry that they should just give up like that. Really, they should just pick themselves up and get on with it. 'Spaniel's ears' is not just an expression now, it's a reality.

2 August

Dave is working constantly in the restaurants, but most of the time he still manages to look after Louis when I'm doing my radio stuff. This morning when I go in, though, someone gamely points out that I have bird shit in my hair. On closer inspection I discover it isn't actually bird shit but banana, which has dried into an interesting colour and consistency. Very Greta Garbo.

4 August

Kirsty and cousin Amy around today. She's now one-and-a-bit and so is up and about. Determined not to be left behind, Louis stands up by clutching on to and hanging off things. He can cruise between tables and chairs as long as there's constant support, but if he lets go for even a second, he falls like a stone, bottom first, on to the ground. Seeing Amy doing her stuff, though, clearly impresses him.

Kirsty and I have a good catch-up as we feed the babies some sausages and watch as the two cousins sit and baby talk to each other. As if to make a point, Amy gently puts her hand up to Louis's face, who gently takes it in his own hand. How sweet, we think. That is, until he stuffs it into his mouth and bites down. Hard. The blood-curdling scream from Amy confirms that this is no love bite and it's soon magnified by a hundred per cent because Louis gets such a shock that he joins in too! God, have we bred a cannibal? I apologise profusely and wonder if I should phone Auntie Joyce. She used to have a muzzle for her Alsatian. Maybe I could borrow it.

5 August

Louis now bangs things together all the time so he can be sure of making a noise that is way out of proportion to his size. When he puts his weapons down, I think, 'Ah, peace and quiet,' but this is when he starts talking. In fact, for hours on end he'll just talk non-stop. It is, of course, complete gibberish, which he delivers meaningfully whilst waving his arms around like some mad Italian delicatessen owner. Maybe it's Italian?

6 August

Give Louis a bottle this morning. He lies there looking at me intensely. I wonder briefly if he's eyeing up my extremities for a chew, but as he finishes his bottle and struggles to sit up on my lap, he turns to face me, grabs my cheeks hard with his two pudgy hands and says, 'Mama.' I'm convinced he knows what he's saying.

I grin broadly at him and say, 'Yes! Yes! Ma-ma,' so he says it again. This continues for about fifteen minutes until he gets bored. I'm not bored. I could listen to it all day.

6 p.m.

Dave arrives home and I meet him at the door.

'He knows I'm his mother,' I announce grandly.

Dave rolls his eyes. 'Of course he knows you're his mother. Who else does he think has been hanging around the house all this time?'

'No, he can say "Mama"!' I explain and drag him through to the lounge where the bathed and cleansed prodigy is sitting playing with his wooden blocks.

David goes over, picks him up and gives him a big bear hug – at which point Louis turns round, stares into his eyes and says, 'Mama.'

Sadly, before I can stop myself, I begin dancing around beside him, pointing at myself going, 'No, I'm Ma-ma, Ma-ma, Ma-ma!'

His big gummy smile almost breaks his face as he turns to David and presses his head on to his father's shoulder as if to say, 'Take me away from this woman. She's wearing me down.'

Mmmm, so I may have jumped the gun a bit.

12 August

I played the piano a lot when Louis was in my tummy and now I play it most days. It always seems to interest him. Today he listens as usual and then, halfway through some boogie-woogie, he grabs the coffee-table, gets up on to his fat little legs and starts bumping up and down. I think he's dancing.

Not wanting to mention it to anyone until he's done it again, I wait till teatime to have it confirmed. There he is in his baby-walker, scooting around the kitchen floor like Torvill or Dean – whichever the male one is – and I put on a CD. He stops, listens and then starts jumping up and down in situ in time to the music. My wee pudding loves music. I'm delighted and convince myself he has a real sense of rhythm.

Nine months old

14 August

Off to see pal Fiona and little Ellen, who is now almost two. The kids are bumbling around quite happily, so we leave them for a moment whilst we go and put the kettle on.

Did you know it only takes two minutes to paint the inside of a baby's ear with nail varnish? No, neither did I. But that's the length of time we leave them in the room, and quite where the nail varnish came from I don't know. At least it's not Chanel Noir, I suppose, but an appropriate shell pink – and it may catch on. Louis quite likes it and Ellen just loves it. I only hope it'll wear off in time. I don't fancy pouring nail varnish remover in there.

21 August

Mum and Dad are down from Aberdeen. They notice a huge difference in Louis – not just in the size of him but in his latest tricks. I suppose over the last few days I've got used to Louis bobbing and banging about in time to music. My dad, a fellow musician, is highly impressed and starts calling Louis 'Buddy Rich'. Only the most famous and talented drummer in the world in the '50s, so no pressure on our wee boy there then!

22 August

Mum's changing Buddy's nappy and I'm wittering on as usual. After she's changed him, she picks him up to give him a big kiss and he gives her a big hard bite.

She puts him down immediately, gives him a very stern look and says, 'No!'

'God, I'm sorry,' I say.

'Och, not to worry,' she says. 'You did that quite a lot too, actually.'

'How did you stop me?'

'Bit you back.'

'What?'

'Bit you back. You never did it again.'

OK, so will steel myself to do that next time.

30 August

Mum and Dad leave today. Louis hasn't bitten since the day he tried to take a chunk out of Mum. I relax my guard and, as I rumble him around after his bath tonight, wrapped up in a towel with his head poking out one end and his feet poking out the other, I lean over to give him a cuddle and he gets my arm. Aaargh! It's bloody sore.

I say, 'NO!' very loudly and then remember my instructions to bite him back. I take his fat pudgy arm in my hand and look at it. And give it a kiss instead and put it back. I can't bite him, I just can't.

As I sit here thinking how pathetic I am as a human discipline machine, he rolls over to me, strokes my face and says, 'Mama.' Huh, I've heard that before! I get up and start tidying the room when he says it again in a much more, 'Hey you, Mother' sort of way. He's definitely saying 'Mama' to me – at last.

David comes home and is yet again informed that he's calling me 'Mama'. He looks unconvinced until Louis has had his bottle and is lying in bed, wrapped in his ga-ga – a purple blanket from Mothercare. It's not even wool. It's sort of acrylic and glow-in-the-dark. But he loves it. He'll not sleep without it. It's his 'ga-ga'. He rolls himself around in it, sucks it, wraps his toys in it and, when I wash it, he hates it until he's dragged it around the carpets for a couple of hours and it's picked up a selection of musty odours again. Lovely.

Louis turns a sleepy eye to Dave and says in his most meaning-ful tone, 'Dada.' Well, now he believes it!

1 September

When people meet me with Louis on the street, they keep asking me my daughter's name so I suppose it must be time to get Louis's hair cut for the first time. Whether it's memories of my cast-off seersucker dress when he was first born or the long eyelashes, I don't know, but I don't want to make life any harder than it already is.

When I was a wee girl I had my hair cut courtesy of my

mother and a device called the Ronco Hair Trimmer. This instrument of torture was advertised on TV and consisted of a razor blade encased by comb-shaped teeth. You combed it through your hair and, as you did so, you'd give yourself – or your unfortunate child, in my case – a radical trim.

Mum loved it and so, as a result, for years I basically looked like a little boy with a very bad haircut. I used to go on errands to the post office and as I stood in the queue I'd inevitably be asked, 'OK, laddie, what can I do for you today!' At which point I'd protest loudly, 'I'm not a laddie. I'm a *lassie!*' They always apologised and then the next time the same thing would happen.

This probably explains why I haven't had my hair cut since 1973 and took great pleasure in binning the Ronco Hair Trimmer as soon as I was old enough to lay blame at the right door. In fact, so upset was I about my hair – or lack of it – that I distinctly remember asking Santa for a wig. A hint that the more astute parent would've taken that I wasn't overly keen on looking like a skelped arse. The joy when I woke that Christmas morning to find that Santa had brought me a long, squaw-like wig was indescribable. Though joy is not the emotion I now experience when I look back at the photos of that stage in my life in which, at all times of the night and day, I'm wearing that bloody wig.

No such torture for Louis, though. He's getting a trim and will look like what he is – a boy.

I take him down to my pal Derek's salon. He's a great hairdresser and very patient, which turns out to be just as well. As soon as Derek produces his scissors, Louis starts thrashing around like a mad man. He's having none of it.

Eventually I get him in a headlock and Derek manages to snip off the longest bits, but it's far from a short back and sides. As a matter of fact, it's more reminiscent of Rod Stewart in his 'Maggie May' era – a feather cut, I think it's called. Still, better than cutting his ears off, I suppose.

3 September
12 stone 1 pound

Have just realised how soon it is until we go on holiday and I've forgotten to stop eating and become a sylph-like supermodel. Aaargh!

Go shopping for summer stuff. The last hot holiday we had ended up in my massive guilt trip over binging whilst pregnant. I buy the essentials, by which time I realise that there's hardly going to be any space left in the case for any of Dave's and my clothes. The sun creams, the hat, the parasol, the buggy, the nappies, the sun-proof clothes, the first-aid kit, the travel cot, the bedding . . .

I'm quite relieved that there's hardly any room left for my stuff as none of it fits me. I have lost a bit of weight just running around after this boy, but I'm still on the hefty side, to say the least. I decide to head off into town to buy a swimsuit and a pair of shorts. That's all I'll need.

2 p.m.

Don't want to go on holiday now. Leave Louis with Kirsty and cousin Amy and go into M&S. Find a swimsuit. It's black and looks like it'll be very flattering, with various bits of Lyrca in all the necessary places. I then make the heinous mistake of trying it on in the overhead-lit changing-rooms. The view from behind is too horrible to contemplate. It looks as though someone has forced me into a pair of white lacy tights, rolled up lots of paper and stuffed it down each leg. There is not even one muscle in those legs and the over-all effect is repulsive. Deeply pissed off.

4.30 p.m.

Go back to collect Louis. Amy's howling.

'Is she all right?' I ask.

It's gently broken to me that I may in fact have given birth to Hannibal Lecter. It seems that Louis is continuing with his strange new habit of eating people. Not so much eating, as tasting by way of a rather nasty bite. A quick snack. Luckily, it seems he doesn't want to go the whole hog and swallow them, but the bite he's now administering is quite impressive and most embarrassing. I'm reliably told it's a phase. Yes, well, they probably said that to Hannibal's mother and look what happened to him.

4 September

Start a diet today. But before I begin in earnest, I think I'd better empty the cupboards of all fattening food. Whilst I'm at it, I might as well eat it 'cos I hate wastage.

Now I feel sick – the perfect way to start a diet, I suppose. I've scoffed a tin of condensed milk, a half-eaten box of Milk Tray that was hidden by me during my last diet attempt, some Hobnobs and a massive packet of nuts. The nuts weren't actually open, but I thought it was a crime to throw them out so I felt I was doing my conscience – if not my thighs – a favour.

5 September

Absolutely starving. Have one Weetabix for breakfast and then stare at Louis's toast like a real saddo. Am determined to give it a shot, though with less than two weeks till we go away, it's probably too little, too late.

I wonder if I can get through ten days in Spain without taking my clothes off? I doubt it.

6 September

Louis has adopted the banana as his favourite food. Thank the Lord for the original fast food. They're not fattening either compared to the usual rubbish I eat, so I go to the cash-and-carry and buy bunches of the darn things to keep round the house. In fact, just like when I was pregnant I always keep one close by in case of emergency. Handbag, car, pocket. When hunger hits, I eat one, and Louis starts by shoving bits of it in his mouth, before he rubs it all over his face, hair, clothes and anybody else who happens to be around.

7 September

Speak to friends who've done holidays abroad with babies. Firstly, they laugh at me for thinking that I'm actually going to have a 'holiday' and then, when eventually they regain control, they give me a few tips. 'Don't go – ha, ha, ha!' Other than that, it's forget the holidays of the past; forget the days of lying on loungers, reading books and occasionally lifting your arm so that someone can see that you are in need of a cold libation. It's not going to be like that in any more, OK?

The tips from the top are: don't leave home without Calpol; and, on the day we travel, keep Louis awake all day in the hope that he'll sleep during the journey. Sounds like a good plan.

8 September

8 p.m.

We're off to Spain. Ten whole days away. Yahoo!

Dave lugs the huge case down to the car as I continually prod Louis to keep him awake. It's very late and the wee man is understandably grumpy.

I now know why the flight was so cheap. It arrives in Alicante at 2 a.m. We arrive at the airport, where we check in and spend two hours shuffling round. By the time we board the plane, we're fraught, as no other sane person with a young child is travelling at this time of night. No, it's more your Club 18–30s on this flight and they're having a rip-roaringly good time at the bar as we pace with buggy and child.

Eventually our flight is called and we're shown to our seats. Louis is under two so he'll sit on one of our knees. Dave gets the short straw. He sits down and then we get Louis strapped in too. In fact, the second his belt is secured, the wee man drops off. Just like that! Dave and I congratulate ourselves on our well-executed plan and as soon as we're airborne decide to order a large drink to celebrate.

We taxi, we take off and, just as the seatbelt sign pings off, Louis suddenly wakes up and starts screeching! Why? I don't bloody know. Dave jiggles him about, we pull faces, I produce a banana but, no matter what we do, he just won't stop. After a few minutes of dirty looks from the Club 18–30s, the hostess comes to our rescue, telling us kids quite often have problems with their ears. It's something to do with the cabin pressure. It's obvious – the wee soul's in agony. The hostess tries to get him to suck a sweetie, which goes down his throat and damn near chokes him – which makes him even more hysterical.

About thirty minutes into the flight, my nerves are in tatters so I make my way to the toilet and just sit there on my own for five minutes, deep breathing. The disapproving looks of the people without kids who'd probably prefer to have us travel in the hold are all around. I used to be one of them, but now I'm on the other side.

On the way back to my seat I make a concerted effort not to grab the trolley from the air-hostess and horse the entire miniature gin collection. Bloody hell! Travelling with a baby's another adventure I'm patently unprepared to deal with.

9 September
2 a.m.

Only once the plane begins its descent into Alicante does Louis cease crying. He's never cried so long and so hard. The moment we're on the ground, he falls into a deep sleep.

Clearing customs, we're optimistic and excited despite ourselves and agree it's wonderful to be in a hot country. We pick up the hire car and drive for an hour in the opposite direction to the one we should be going in due to my appalling map-reading, but even that doesn't matter because at last the baby's asleep and peaceful in the back.

4 a.m.

Arrive at our villa. It looks great, even though it's pitch dark. We manage to get Louis out of the car seat and into his travel cot without waking him up. Amazingly. We just about get our stuff in from the car before we too collapse into an exhausted heap. Thank goodness we've arrived.

5.45 a.m.

Louis awakes so we all get up, desperate to see where we are now the sun is up. Boy, is it up! It's absolutely boiling. There's no way I can wander about in jeans in this heat, so I eventually take the plunge and get into the summer gear. We hold Louis down and clart him in factor 30 – which takes ages – and then we strap him into his buggy and off we go. We walk into the town of Javea, stopping every five or ten yards as I adjust the parasol over the buggy. It's so hot I'm convinced the baby'll burn.

We arrive at the beach front, which is peppered with bars and restaurants and shops selling large inflatable sharks and beach mats. The smell of heat and coffee is everywhere and we're all very happy as we park up and order ice creams for breakfast! Why not.

Run into a woman called Edith from Scotland. Her baby is a couple of months younger than Louis. As we chat, she glances at her wee one, who starts making the unmistakable noises and faces of an imminent bowel movement. His face screws up like a hanky and becomes progressively more purple as the act continues.

Eventually there's a look of relief as shit shoots out of everywhere. Rather than take the calm and book-like approach to the situation, Edith stands up, grabs the pram and just begins running towards the sea. We all watch with our mouths open when she hits the water and just keeps running until her, the pram and the baby are all semi-submerged. She laughs, the baby laughs, the effluence floats away and we continue as normal. Well, sort of. She's clearly barking. I like this woman.

As we sit looking out over the beach and the Mediterranean Sea, we agree the whole atmosphere here is so relaxing even I may chill out. We do a supermarket run for food, mosquito coil and loo rolls and then decide to take Louis to the beach. Theory great – practice a bloody nightmare. Unable to walk, he crawls along in the sand. As soon as the heat from the sand – which is immense – travels through his skin, he squawks and we lift him back on to his beach towel. There he sits for a couple of minutes, before doing exactly the same thing again. Once he realises that sand burns his legs, he decides instead to eat it. And so he spends the rest of the afternoon getting sand in his eyes and ears and up his nose. Not for five minutes do David and I manage just to lie prostrate in the sun, eyes closed, relaxing. It seems Jeffy was right.

All go to bed early, exhausted.

10 September

Baby hasn't slept. Neither have I. He's too hot and wriggling about. I can't take his nappy off or he'll pee everywhere so I lie awake eyeing him eyeing me as Dave sleeps like a baby. Whoever coined the phrase 'sleeping like a baby' wants slapping.

The villa is part of a complex with a communal pool. Today we decide to stay here, primarily because we haven't got the energy to go anywhere else. There's a five-minute break whilst Dave bobs around with the wee man in his rubber-ring seat. Heaven.

11 September

Routine gone to rat shit. Louis clearly doesn't like the heat and is determined to spend his nights like a miniature hippo, rumbling around trying to get out of his cot and into our bed. Aware of other people in the vicinity, I do my best to try and keep him quiet. Am so desperate that I end up in the cot like a contortionist – Louis curled up into a ball in the corner, Dave spread-eagled on the bed snoring his head off. Grrrrr.

2 a.m.

Must have dropped off eventually 'cos I'm rudely awoken by Louis crying his eyes out. He's very hot. Dave suggests it's 'cos I'm squashing him. I give him the evil eye as I point out that without me in here he'd be creating merry hell all bloody night and would he like to explain that to the holidaymakers who – luckily for them – live in the other half of the villa? Dave takes this on board quickly, which is just as well.

Worryingly, once the argument dies down we can hear Louis breathing in short, rasping breaths. Almost instantly he's developed a very bad wheezy chest. We both sit up with him and, by the time morning comes, he's had two lots of Calpol and is in a terrible state. Even breathing normally he sounds like a ninety-year-old chain-smoker with emphysema.

Unanimously, we decide to take him to the local doctor, who examines him thoroughly and sits us down to tell us he has bronchial pneumonia. I can't believe my ears. My little baby boy. I want to go home.

We're told to keep him inside, out of the sun and quiet.

Is there nothing else we can do?

He gives us some antibiotics and tells us, no, there's not.

I want to ask if he might die, but I can't. I'm too afraid of the answer. Instead, I choose to go to pieces and we take turns doing a twenty-four-hour vigil by the side of our poor hot, wheezy child.

Ten months old

12 September

Dave goes off to the travel agent in the town to try and get us home, but it seems there are no flights available. We have no choice but to administer his antibiotics and stay inside the villa panicking. Nothing we can do. We take turns sitting with him during the night, and the daylight hours are spent curled up on the couch worrying, reading books and eating.

18 September

The past few days have just been hell. Sitting in the house doing nothing but watching Louis for signs of improvement. We go home tomorrow, thank God. Last night he slept for three hours in a row, which is the most he's managed since he got this terrible infection. His appetite even shows signs of returning as he grabs a baguette from my handbag and jams it into his mouth. I think he's turned the corner. I can't wait to get back home.

19 September

We check into the airport early and, despite the fact we're desperate to get back to Scotland, I'm dreading the flight and hoping against all odds that Louis's ears will be fine.

As we take off, I feel tears rolling down my face. I'm so relieved we're on our way and scared Louis's ears will go. After half an hour it's apparent things are going to be OK, thank God. It's only now I relax slightly, until it dawns on me that I'm trapped between David – with Louis on his knee – on one side and an exceedingly fat man scared of flying on the other. This man sweats more than any human being I've ever seen. His great rolls of extra flesh hang over his seat and flop over our communal armrest.

I spend most of the flight talking to him and convincing him that we're not going to plummet from the sky and die in a hideous plane crash. He's from Bo'ness and halfway through the flight a woman turns up from the back of the plane to talk to him.

'You a'right, Jim?' she asks.

'Oh aye, hen, I'll be fine noo,' he answers.

'Could you not get a seat together?' I ask sympathetically.

'Oh aye, but she winnae sit aside me 'cos I'm that fat and sweaty!' He laughs. He would.

Arrive home – delighted to be back but utterly exhausted.

My pal Fiona picks us up at the airport. 'You look bloody awful!' she says. 'Oh, and happy birthday!' Thanks. I'd forgotten.

20 September

Definition of holiday: a period spent away from work or duty; a period of recreation. Ha, ha, ha.

It's wonderful to be back home. Back in a country where we understand what's going on and know where to find things. Back near a chemist that sells drugs in bottles we can read. And back to a doctor who speaks English.

We make an appointment for first thing tomorrow and spend the rest of the day wandering about, appreciating small things like the telephone and cold weather.

21 September

Off to the doctor where, after a prod, a tickle and a listen to his chest, he concludes that Louis has indeed got a bad chest infection.

'Bronchial pneumonia?' I ask.

'Possible but unlikely,' he says. Much as I'd like to sue the doctor in Spain for putting us through such mental torture, I'm too relieved that, despite what we were told, Louis most likely did not have a life-threatening illness after all.

Get back from the surgery feeling much happier. There's a message from STV asking me to present a new chat-show. The euphoria is short-lived when I realise they want to meet me tomorrow and I've no childcare, a sickly white face and the body of a Teletubby.

22 September

Off to Glasgow to meet the producer about the new TV series. Get on the train to Glasgow. Am an hour early so wander around Buchanan Street. The Glasgow girls are so stylish, trendy and groovy that I suffer a crisis of confidence. Looking at the off-white shirt and ancient blue linen trousers I'm wearing, I realise I need something new to wear. Have a mad dash round the shops and find a dark-brown suit in Jigsaw with a jacket so long it hides many a buttock-related sin.

Arrive to meet the producer with my confidence marginally restored. First thing she asks is, 'Shall we go and have some lunch?' What an excellent start. So we discuss the show over some great food and then, having sealed the deal, emerge into daylight. We continue walking along and talking until we're about to cross the road when a fire engine whizzes by. Before I can check herself, my arm is up, my finger's pointing and I'm staring and grinning maniacally into the producer's eyes shouting, 'Nee-naw! Nee-naw!' Pointing out fire engines to top TV producers? Oh dear, dear, dear. Want to die. Spend the journey home on the train cringing.

23 September

Girls round for lunch. They end themselves laughing when I tell them my fire engine story. I'm soon feeling better when Jeffy – who's a CA – confesses that, just after she went back to work after having her baby, she was in a meeting with her chairman organising an audit and, before they left to go back to their office on the other side of town, she inadvertently asked him if he needed to go to the loo before they set off. Wonderful. I'm not alone. Then Kath tells me she was walking along a street and, when they were about to cross, she grabbed her colleague's hand saying, 'Careful, darling, it's a busy, *busy* road.'

24 September

Get a call from the producer. The job is mine – as long as I promise not to point out all the fast red engines that whizz past us during filming. I accept the conditions with an appropriately red face and know I must stop eating now. The show goes out live on Thursday nights at 10.30 p.m. It's called *Late Edition* and I'll have to be in Glasgow all day on Tuesdays, Wednesdays and Thursdays for rehearsals, scripting and research. Great. Now I've to address the diet *and* childcare issues. I've no choice.

25 September
11 stone 12 pounds

Start making enquiries about diets and childcare. Blimey! I've a lot to do in a few weeks.

Diet starts in earnest today. The thought of being on live TV should bring on the trots, frankly, and get my heart rate up to an impressive, calorie-burning rate. Decide on Rosemary Conley. She's worked in the past – the lots-of-food-but-no-fat diet. OK, that's the easy part. Finding the right person to look after my cheeky wee pudding is another thing altogether.

29 September

Jogging – and drizzling down the tracksuit bottoms. At last I understand what the pelvic floor is all about. It's just too late for mine.

5 October

Make an appointment to go and meet childminder no. 1. Can't believe my luck. She's a lovely woman, she lives in a small house which is spotlessly clean and she's licensed to look after four kids, with her own six-year-old at school. I take to her immediately. She's an Irish girl with the sort of house I always like to think that I'll have one day – sort of warm, organised, co-ordinated and comfortable, with the waft of baking and coffee in the air. My Doris Day instinct tells me that this is the one.

Delighted with how easy this whole thing has been, I tell her of my decision. She smiles apologetically and explains that she's very flattered but she has a waiting-list of three other children already, but if I'd like to put Louis's name down I'd be very welcome. So he might get in when he's about fifteen.

Say goodbye and continue the search.

7 October

Am given the name and number of a woman who, although she isn't a registered childminder, has years and years of experience. Willing to at least meet her, off I go.

The moment she opens her front door, I think – in a most unchristian way – 'harridan'. She wears a scruffy, frayed housecoat and there's eau de fag everywhere. This is confirmed when I clock the fag butts accumulated on her back step, which she does her best to avoid showing me. As if being a chain-smoker isn't enough to deter me, when I ask to see her garden I realise it's more than just fags I'm smelling. But it's not until I see the culprits that I'm able to identify that sour and unmistakable odour. I've lived in too many tenement stairs not to know cat piss when it hits me between the eyes, and to say this woman likes cats is an understatement. Looking at the selection of sly-eyed creatures lounging around her garden and kitchen, I think she'd be better suited as an extension to the cat and dog home rather than caring for children. This is confirmed when one of the sly wee scratchers ambles past and one of the children in her care makes a determined swipe to grab the cat's tail – a natural reaction which I myself have to curb, even at this mature stage in life. Anyway, the harridan swoops down, plucking the cat up into her arms to protect it from the child whilst berating the wee girl not to hurt Kitty or Kitty might just hurt her – which, incidentally, would serve her right. Time to go.

8 October

Decide that perhaps childminders aren't going to be the answer, so investigate some nurseries instead. There are so many, it's hard to know where to start. I leave Louis with his grandma and go for a scout, starting with somewhere quite close to where we live. I mean, why make life harder than it already is?

The nursery is in a large, old Edinburgh house. Very impressive from the outside, but inside it's damp, dark and smells terrible. The girl showing me round is suffering from a severe lack of enthusiasm and, when we go into the 'playroom', it's obvious that this is just someone's big old family house that they can't afford to keep without the nursery scam to generate some extra cash. The 'playroom' is basically a library in everything but name. There are shelves and shelves of books, all dusty and unread, lining the not insubstantial walls from floor to ceiling. In the middle of this is a grotty, dark carpet on which lie a selection of Lego bricks and kids. It just looks dirty, dusty and revolting.

Still keeping an open mind – well, sort of – we go into the next room. This is a glass conservatory which, due to the pelting rain outside, is leaking rather effusively all over the place. As if this isn't bad enough, in conjunction with the drizzly water dripping in, they have a water-play area which is being enthusiastically utilised by several of the wee toddlers. This isn't the problem. The problem is that, to keep them warm, there's an electric bar heater right next to them . . . with all four bars burning hot orange. From the back of it, the flex snakes up and over several of the surrounding implements and toys. Electricity, water and kids. Death-trap nursery.

Leave feeling a bit sick. It's an accident waiting to happen. Phone Social Services and report them.

☽ ☆October

From one extreme to the other. Arrive at the next nursery, where the woman looks like someone has removed her brain. She speaks to everyone – adults and children alike – as if they're two. She has a sing-song voice which soothes me. I like this place. I have a good look round. It's light, bright and clean, with lots of brightly coloured walls and toys.

We walk into the back room, where there's a yellow-looking child lying on a beanbag.

'What's wrong with him?' I ask.

'Oh, he's been sick.'

'What about his parents? Are they coming to get him?' I ask, looking at the snivelling wee thing.

'Oh, he'll be fine. You'll soon buck up, won't you, Sam?' she say to the listless, pale-faced, ill boy.

Basic human right of being reunited with parent at earliest opportunity denied. I'm out of here. My first instinct that someone's removed her brain may be true after all. Forget it!

Take Louis back home for lunch and then off I go again. This time the nursery is populated by blokes – and I don't mean the babies, I mean the carers. Now, I'm mature and I not only believe passionately in sexual equality, but I've bumped my gums about it for years. One day I even hope to get paid half as much as the blokes who do exactly the same damn job as I do. However, until then I'd prefer some soft-haired, sweet-natured young girl to be caring for my child, not a bloke with hands the size of meat cleavers and a twelve o'clock shadow. I'm sorry, I love men – God knows that this is exactly how I got to be in this position in the first place – but there's a little part of me that is not a hundred per cent about them there lads being in a full-time baby-caring job. Would your dad, your grandad, your brother? Mmmm, mine neither. Exactly.

Have one more nursery to check out on the way home. I walk in and am offered a glass of wine. Take it, but if they're doling out the drink to everyone who piles through the door, they'll be half-cut by teatime. Leave after another glass and a few crisps. Nice place for a drink, but as a serious childcare possibility? I don't think so.

Am getting a little despondent to say the least. What does the rest of the world do?

Eleven months old

25 October

Time is running out. I must find the right place. Someone has just opened up a new nursery so I dash off to see it.

Everyone here is in such starched uniforms that, if one of the kids fell over, the staff would have difficulty bending down to help them up. They look like they'd just declare, 'Stuff and nonsense!' and tell the wee soul to buck up and get on with it whilst stemming the flow of blood from the gaping wound with the end of a squeegee.

The formidable woman who runs the place is terrifying, and that's to me – a grown adult! As I'm shown around, I keep checking myself to make sure that I'm not slouching and answer 'Yes' instead of 'Yeh' or 'Uh-huh', and feel like I'm being auditioned to join a military task force. As I march out in an upright fashion, I glance at the date on top of the newspaper, thinking that perhaps I've entered a time-warp. But no, it reads this millennium.

Say goodbye, resist clicking my heels together and ruminate in the car with a bag of Minstrels. This nursery thing is a lot bloody harder than I thought. It'd be fair to say that, up to this point in my life, I haven't even been able to select a cleaner successfully, let alone someone I can trust to look after my wee pudding – and the criteria in this instance are a modicum more important than being able to wield a can of Pledge. I'm now questioning my never-before questioned ability to read people. I suppose it's never mattered so much, especially with my track record. I remember thinking Rebecca De Mornay was lovely, and look what she did in *The Hand that Rocks the Cradle*! Bollocks. I wish I hadn't remembered that film. Now I'll suspect everyone of being a psychopath. Secretly suspect it's me that's the psychopath and barking after all.

27 October
11 stone 10 pounds

At last I've found the perfect nursery . . . but they won't take kids till they're two-and-a-half – or at least past the nappy stage. Am quite despondent about this.

My face must be telling the story 'cos as I'm leaving one of the women says to me, 'Actually, a lovely girl applied here for a job and we would love to have taken her on but we're full at the moment. I could give you her number, if you like?'

I gratefully accept it and then go home to try and call.

28 October

I phone her and she comes round this morning. She's called Julie and she's the soft-haired, sweet girl I always envisaged would look after Louis whilst I go off to work. She's training to be a teacher and is a natural with kids. We're delighted to have found her and very lucky – and the best thing about it is, Louis adores her at first sight. She'll start this weekend whilst I do my radio stuff and then, in a couple of weeks when the TV programme starts, she'll be here for three days a week. At last I may be about to launch myself back into the working world.

6 November
11 stone 8 pounds

Spend my days rushing between Glasgow and Edinburgh on the train. Just this level of rushing around seems to have kicked my metabolic rate up and I've lost a few pounds – which is just as well as the show starts in less than a week.

Julie is working out brilliantly. She's like one of the family already. She doesn't bat an eyelid at the mess, the muddle, the noise, Bone Dog, or David and me rushing about half-dressed, trying to get going in the morning. She's a real find. Louis is so happy when she arrives in the morning that he speed-crawls to her knee and just sits there grinning madly.

10 November

Frantic week. Programme starts tomorrow night. Through in Glasgow both yesterday and today.

The set is in the main studio. There's a live studio audience and, as the show's at 10.30 at night, the chances are they'll have had a few drinks. Incredibly nervous. Not only have I not done TV for two years but I've never done it live. Live radio is fine but – gulp – on television . . .

The guests are great. They include Richard Wilson – a.k.a. Victor Meldrew – Noddy Holder from Slade and Midge Ure. The research was produced yesterday and I've been reading it until my eyes are red and my head is spinning. I'm as ready as I'll ever be.

11 November
8 a.m.
Show time!

Julie arrives early so that I can head to off Glasgow. The whole day is spent rehearsing and reworking lines.

6 p.m.
In hair and make-up.

8 p.m.
A full rehearsal. It all goes very well indeed.

10 p.m.
The audience is in situ and I'm shaking with nerves and going to the loo a lot. I phone home to check on the wee man, feeling terribly guilty that I've been so damn busy I haven't given him or anyone a second thought all day. Bad, evil mother, I think as I get ready to walk down to the studio.

The warm-up man is on and has the audience roaring with laughter as I stand in the wings with a knot in my stomach and a heart rate dangerously high for a woman of my tender years.

Suddenly we're on. I sit on the couch in my designated spot. The audience are so close I can feel them breathing down my neck. I feel sick.

Our first guest is Richard Wilson. I've heard he can be challenging sometimes so I've read up on him and his career thoroughly. As he sits down, I introduce him.

The conversation goes well until I mention the fact that he's just finished a play at The Theatre Royal in London. It turns out that the research notes are wrong and it's thirteen months since he did that play. So at this point he has a choice: ignore it and move on, or bring it up. He choses the latter.

'It's a shame you haven't done your research, dear,' he says. 'That was over a year ago.'

I think I'm going to be sick. I feel stupid and useless and I want to leave. To the best of my ability, I laugh it off, but inside I'm petrified. What else will go wrong?

As it turns out nothing. It all goes brilliantly and the consensus of opinion is that he was just a bit tough on me. Still feel crap, though.

12 November

The newspapers review the show. There are several really great ones, but the *Daily Star* picks up the Richard Wilson moment and makes me seem like an incompetent fool.

Shuffle around for a while – the way you'd expect an incompetent fool to – until my pal, Dynamite Di, phones and demands that I go to the pub, where we plot and scheme and laugh the night away.

One year old!

13 November

Louis's first birthday.

Good grief! He's survived having us as parents for a whole year. It's the longest, most remarkable year I've ever had. But it's only taken a moment to go by and it's hard to believe how different we all were this time last year. I think I've grown up a lot. Dave disagrees. He thinks *he's* grown up a lot. I disagree.

So maybe neither of us have, but one thing's for sure: little Louis Alexander Mackie Scott has. He's now a standing up, bouncing up and down, smiley, shiny-haired, sparky, brown-eyed boy – a.k.a. the light of my life.

Invite lots of babies and their mums around for a wee party. I've never baked a cake before in my puff, but decide that today's the day to do it. It takes me hours, it sags in the middle and the kitchen looks like a bomb's hit it, but I do it. As all the bobbly-headed babies, rampaging toddlers and bemused parents eat crisps, I march in with my cake feeling ridiculously pleased with myself. It's amazing what can happen in 365 short little days.

16 November

At last seem to be getting into a rhythm with the show. Three days a week I'm in Glasgow and Louis is with Julie. He loves her and vice versa. At weekends when I'm doing the radio programme, David steps into the breach, so Louis is well cared for at all times and life can continue with a semblance of order.

10 December

Louis was at one of his wee squishy friend's birthday parties today. He rumbled about and poked his fingers into things and people as per usual. As we leave, he's handed a party bag. Opening it when we get home, there's a car in it. He's ecstatic. A car. He's had it clutched in his sticky paw since he got it and thinks it's the most wonderful thing he's ever seen. Nature or nurture? I think we know the answer now.

16 December

Final show of *Late Edition* in the current run. Have a bosker of a last show. Great fun. Great atmosphere. And afterwards we go upstairs to have a few drinks. My chum Dynamite is chatting to some bloke who's a real laugh.

'Have you ever thought about TV yourself?' she asks.

'Well . . .' he replies.

'Well,' she says, 'if you get your hair cut and lose a bit of weight, you could do it – you're bloody funny, you know.'

It isn't till later it transpires she'd been talking to the Director of Light Entertainment for STV. Gulp. There goes my career.

17 December

With the show over for the time being, Julie is off the hook. I know plenty of women who have childcare so they can dander about doing things like having lunch or getting a facial, but I can't. There's something about being an Aberdonian who's worked full-time since I was sixteen that doesn't allow me that sort of self-indulgence. I'd just feel guilty about paying someone else to look after Louis when there's no earthly reason why I shouldn't be doing it myself – at least till the next programme comes up.

18 December

Wish I still had Julie. We're having everyone for Christmas this year and I decide to start the Christmas shopping today. I'm getting nowhere fast. Clutching my list, we're ready to go and, just before we leave, Louis does a giant poo which has to be dealt with.

The second attempt to depart is foiled by the fact that he gets hold of a big squishy pear, which he squeezes hard until it explodes – all over him, all over me and all over my hair.

Attempt three. He's obviously hungry, having wasted the pear on interior decoration, so he grizzles in the car. Stop at a garage and buy a packet of biscuits for him to eat. Eventually get to the Gyle Shopping Centre . . . without the list. Go home in a very bad mood after queuing for an hour to get out of the bloody carpark.

20 December
Dave announces he'll get a tree. We don't really discuss what kind. Fake or real?

3.30 p.m.
The doorbell rings and two blokes announce they're here to deliver a tree. I wonder why Dave couldn't have taken it himself – until I see it. It's absolutely *vast*. Not dissimilar to the tree that is gifted to Edinburgh every year by the Norwegians and sits on the Mound for the whole city to enjoy. And just marginally smaller than the Jenners' Christmas tree, which is hoisted in through the roof of the department store and is four storeys high.

By the time the two guys have wrestled it into our lounge and lopped about half of it off so it can be stood upright, I'm speechless. A quick look at Bone Dog shows he's rather pleased. Great, he's obviously thinking, I don't need to go outside anymore to lift my leg. Louis just looks scared of it and, as David walks in through the door, I recognise the expression on his face too – but not so much scared of the tree, no, more of me, his dear wife.

'We'll need to sell the car to afford to decorate this rainforest,' I point out.

'Och, well, it's Louis's first real Christmas. Let's make it a good one.'

So we deck the halls with boughs of paper-chains, and jam the base of the tree in between about twelve bricks retrieved from the garden to save it from falling over as Louis crawls towards it and uses the branches to pull himself up. Finally we open a bottle of wine and toast our forest. Despite my reservations, it looks wonderful.

24 December
2 p.m.

Christmas shopping panic. Leave Louis with David and go into the centre of town. It's hell. The shops are packed, it's freezing outside and boiling inside. The list I've made is useless. I hope for inspiration as I wander around, but I realise I have to put my head down and just barge through everything and everyone in order to get a look in.

Decide to do a one-hit wonder and head for Jenners. I sweat and push with the best of them and, after queuing for eons, manage to escape with a few carrier-bags packed with goodies. Arriving home, I then lock myself in the bedroom for about four hours wrapping. I'm hopeless at wrapping and have a few glasses of wine to make the experience more palatable.

11 p.m.

Have shopped, wrapped and am on my knees. The most important thing of all is the stocking, which I place on the floor by Louis's cot.

25 December

Louis's stocking is an old kilt sock stuffed with funny wee things from the Early Learning Centre. Of course, he has no idea what's going on, but we watch his face as he takes ages unravelling bits of tissue-paper and shrieks with joy at the plastic animal or ball within. It takes hours and watching him suddenly makes me remember the magic of Christmas. This is what it's all about.

Blimey, Christmas is a darn sight better this year than last, I can tell you. I've a chest that doesn't need its own passport, I can genuinely smile again and I've bursts of sleep longer than fifteen minutes. Welcome to the world!

26 December

Boxing Day. As per usual sitting around, over-fed, surrounded by paper and rubbish. Enjoying a temporary lull in all the action, Dave and I are watching back the video footage of yesterday while Louis stands at the coffee-table, hanging on for dear life, when he just turns round, looks at me and, with a face of deep concentration, puts one foot in front of the other. Yes, Louis walks. He takes his first, tentative steps and is now officially a toddler. A monumental day and Dave and I get so excited and make such a noise that the wee soul falls flat on his face. Determined, though, he just gets up and does it again.

4 January

Now that Louis walks – after a fashion – I can start going along to the toddler group with Jeffy. The only condition is that they toddle. Well, this one does, so we arrange to meet at 9.15 to go along together.

The fact that it's in a church hall worries me, as I wonder whether or not there'll be some subliminal early indoctrination into the ways of the Church. It seems not. It's more to do with a frustrated ex-teacher needing to find some nappy-brained adults to boss around as if we were six.

We do as we're told. Sit down, tidy up, go over there, don't walk with your coffee cup, sit down in one of those chairs designed for four-year-olds. Who on earth still has a four-year-old bottom? A thirty-one-year-old bottom that has recently expanded to a remarkable degree, perhaps. Illustrated beautifully by poor Brenda.

Brenda – a tired-looking girl with triplets, no less – gets her coffee and, for fear of incurring the wrath of Brown Owl, duly jams herself into one of the baby chairs. Twenty minutes later and feeling much better for her caffeine injection, she stands up – unfortunately with the chair still snugly hanging on to her bottom. No amount of jiggling and wobbling is going to ease her out. It takes three other mothers – trying not to laugh loudly – to help her out. After the count of three and while one of them holds on to Brenda's arms at the front, the other two pull at the chair as hard as they can from behind. It very much reminds me of Winnie the Pooh stuck in the equivalent of Rabbit's hole – and Brenda, much like Winnie, is finally set free.

As she flies out of the chair she begins to laugh – hard. Eventually everyone joins in until the room is full of hysterical women. It would have been the best laugh I've had in ages had it not brought to my attention how poor my pelvic floor still is. In fact, I might be mistaken, but I'm fairly sure that there's an overwhelming smell of urine as most of the mums in the group lose the plot.

23 January
12 stone 3 pounds again

Julie is back in the house. I've a new programme coming up and so she's to be here every Tuesday and Wednesday. My new show is a cookery programme called *Square Meals*, which is most appropriate for someone who loves her grub as much as I do. Must try and get back in shape.

After the excess of Christmas and New Year, my diet has gone for a Burton. I've done nothing other than eat. I got to the stage where I said to myself, 'Calm down, woman. I mean, how much damage can I do in a few weeks?' The answer is 'Extensive'.

I blame my metabolic rate. It seems to have stopped altogether. I weigh myself and am horrified. The start date for the show is looming. I decide to go for the radical cabbage-soup-diet approach – a quick fix with some rather unpleasant side-effects – i.e. farting like a dray horse. However, drastic measures are required. I boil up a ton of the stuff. I swear it tastes like dung, but I drink it anyway. Stare longingly at Louis as he wolfs down his macaroni cheese. It'll be worth it.

28 January

Every day that I've been working, I come home and Julie's there with Louis. They've always produced something – some biscuits, a painting, a lovely picture made from leaves and cones collected from the park. Every day I try not to look deeply inadequate as a mother. I've never baked – apart from his birthday cake – painted or made any craft stuff with him at all. She's so good with him, I sometimes think he'll just stop loving me and go entirely for her – altogether a much better and more wholesome individual. I can't say I'd blame him, actually.

3 February

No matter what's going on, I like to make the effort to go along to the toddler group. It gets me together with other women in the same boat, and of course it's a fascinating place.

There are three camps:

1. the ones who have baggy eyes, baggy clothes and no idea who they are;
2. the well-dressed, clean and together ones, who clearly have a full-time nanny or a box of Prozac in their bags;
3. the actual nannies, who all huddle together, smiling and whispering amongst themselves and probably thinking, 'God, I won't go to seed like that lot when a baby comes along. It's not going to change my life.' Huh! Been there.

Have also discovered a new breed of human. I've heard of – and witnessed – the smug marrieds, but they don't hold a candle to the smug parents. The unflappable, organic-food-eating, hey-let-it-all-wash-over-you brigade. While I sweat and wriggle with Louis, telling him right from wrong as he stomps up and down and pokes children in the eye, they don't bat an eyelid as their little darlings leap up and down on our coffee-table like whirling dervishes, run full pelt at the dog using him for football practice, and flip the cover of the piano up and thump it as hard as their little hard fists will allow. Personally, I wouldn't stand for it.

19 February

Louis is due for his MMR inoculation. I'm in a total quandary about it. There's so much in the press, I've no idea what's the right thing to do. I talk to friends, colleagues and the doctor. No one can give me a definitive answer. Decide to wait a couple of months to see if there's any clear directive.

24 February

Someone told them at toddler group that I can play the piano. You'd think that, doing TV and radio, it'd be a complete breeze, but it's not. I hate doing things like this in public. I tell them I'd rather not but I'm told by Brown Owl to go up on the stage and get on with it whilst everyone else sings.

I feel like I'm twelve again. This is the school concert (without Gordon chasing me round backstage saying, 'Do you want to see my doo-doo?'). I do as I'm told and sit there upright playing 'Here We Go Round the Mulberry Bush'. I'm blushing furiously. I hate every minute of it. Brown Owl stands clapping in time to the music and I eventually finish with 'Old MacDonald Had a Farm' to rapturous applause from the one-to-three-year-olds. I feel like Barry Manilow. I am Lola and this is my Copacabana.

1 March
11 stone 7 pounds

Get my wardrobe allowance from STV for the cookery shows. We have twenty-five to record. Each day I'll be filming with a top British chef. They'll be cooking and preparing food whilst I talk to them about what they're doing. Can you imagine how happy I am when, talking through the logistics of the show, it dawns on me that I'll only be filmed from the waist up – I use the term 'waist' loosely – so all I need are shirts, T-shirts and some aprons, which I can borrow from Dave's restaurant. Ideal.

3 March

Grab my stylish friend Fiona and an uplift bra from M&S and then hit the shops. My boobs are annoying me a lot and when, just after lunchtime, I stumble into the changing-room in Next, I'm more than pleased to find that the way they cut their shirts suits me perfectly. The assistant's face is a picture when I buy twenty of them. Well, it doesn't need to be Oormani – not if I'm paying.

5 March

Reading through scripts with one eye whilst looking after the wee man. He's in great form just now. He's just learned to walk backwards and spends most of his time doing just that. I'm not sure why. He keeps falling over Bone Dog – who's taken to hiding under the kitchen table looking pissed off – and crashing into walls and doors. But it's his new trick and he's very pleased with himself.

2.30 p.m.

Louis is playing with his cars in the lounge when I suddenly hear a very strange noise. On investigation, it's coming from the phone. Picking up the receiver, I listen – only to hear the emergency services. He's inadvertently dialled 999 and – boy! – do I get a rocket from them. Tell Louis not to touch the phone or Mummy might be incarcerated, which would be a shame as I'm the person who buys the chocolate puddings in this house.

23 March

Ready to go to Glasgow for a week. Each day we aim to record five programmes. We're to start at 8 a.m. and work till we're finished. It'll be long and gruelling, but it'll be great fun.

I've been offered hotel accommodation for the whole time 'cos it'd take a good hour-and-a-half travelling at both ends of the day to get across there and back. Feel guilty about the fact that I'm highly excited about staying in a hotel – on my own with room service, a colour TV and a power shower. Uninterrupted sleep. Hallelujah!

I know I'll miss Louis terribly, but Mum is coming down from Aberdeen to stay and David'll be here, so I say my fond farewells. Before I leave, I Blu-tak on to Louis's bedroom door a photograph that we took of him last Christmas where he's sitting in a cardboard box, to which I add a speech bubble which says, 'Please don't let my dad dress me – *please!*' This has become a running gag in our house. Every time David dresses the wee man, he looks like a refugee whose mother has just fished out any old scraps and patches from the back of a charity lorry. I know that as a general rule men aren't gifted in this area, but when you see your son looking like he should be sleeping in a cardboard box on Princes Street, action has to be taken. I know David'll take it in the spirit in which I make it.

28 March

Spent my whole week in Glasgow. Working, eating and sleeping. Not just sleeping, but long, uninterrupted, dreamless, exhausted, catch-up shut-eye. It's wonderful. I feel great. I speak to Louis every morning and every night. Or at least I talk, and I hear him heavy breathing on the other end of the phone. I miss him terribly, but I'm so loving being in my own room, no noise, nothing, I know I'll return a calmer, more relaxed person.

Getting home is a joy. Seeing my wee pudding, I'm sure he's grown in the five days since I saw him last. Within an hour I also suspect he's been on a training programme, practising the word, 'No!' It's uttered about fifty times between my arrival back and him going off to his bed. This'll be the stamp of his own authority arriving, I suspect. Damn. It was bound to happen sometime.

2 April
11 stone 4 pounds

Due to my absence last week, Brown Owl has found out what I do for a living and has started being sickeningly nice to me at toddler group. After I have my coffee in my miniature chair, it becomes apparent why, when she sidles up to me and announces that it'd be great to arrange a tour around a TV studio for the kids. Is she serious? Having been bossed around by her mercilessly for nigh on three months, I tell her gently that to take twenty toddlers into a TV studio would probably end in electrocution and death – *plus* they're just getting to grips with focusing enough on the TV screen to check out Laa-Laa and Po without needing to see the machinations of what goes on behind the scenes. She clearly hates me now. Fine. The feeling is entirely mutual.

4 April

According to my mum, two of my first words were 'Reginald Bosanquet', the name of the TV newsreader at the time. It must be hereditary because, from the moment he opens his eyes in the morning till the moment they reluctantly close at night, Louis never stops talking. There's no doubt he's going to be a major chatterbox – pointing, sitting on a plastic tractor and, when I ask him to do something, saying, 'No!'

10 April

I've noticed that Louis's eating is getting a bit fussy. He's been like a human disposal unit for months now, to the extent that he'd literally eat anything. I've even tried to catch him out a couple of times. One day I cut up a lemon and put it on the table of his high-chair, just to watch his reaction. He popped it in his mouth as I stood waiting for his face to screw up into a ball. Not in the least. He just munched through it as if it were sweet honeydew melon. Another phase, apparently, is when they start turning their noses up at things. Dave says he'll begin to take strange and unusual food home to tempt him to keep trying new things. A good idea.

11 April

True to his word, David comes home with some small orange fruits which have little papery leaves. They're called physalis or Japanese Lanterns. I wash a few and put them on a plate for Louis. He eyes them and then eats one. He loves them and polishes off the lot. Good, this seems to be going well.

14 April

Going round Sainsbury's with Louis standing in the trolley,

talking as usual. He's pointing and grabbing anything that takes his fancy as we whizz past. Just as we're at the fruit and veg section, he spots his new favourite fruit, points and shouts, 'Syphilis! Syphilis! I want syphilis!' I swear I'll kill David if I survive long enough to get home.

3 May
11 stone

David has announced that we're going off to Ireland for a holiday. 'Holiday' is a word that used to whip me into a frenzy, but after our last experience it'd be fair to say that the thought hardly causes a frisson of excitement.

We aim to head off in time for our anniversary, which will be lovely. And at least it won't be too hot and we can get home if we want to. Yes, I think paranoia would be a good description of how I'm feeling about such things after Spain last year.

7 May

Punching and pushing. Lovely. He's never seen a violent video unless the uncut, late-night edition of *The Teletubbies* has sneaked into his video collection. But I can't see Po and Dipsy panelling one another. Where it comes from, who knows? But he's enjoying a good bit of rough and tumble at the moment. I don't mind, actually. I'd rather he was a rough-and-tumbler than a sit-stiller, but there must be a happy medium.

Eighteen months old

15 May

It's funny how quickly things change. Right after you have a baby, everyone and anyone who has a baby is a comrade. We've been there, done that and got the stretch marks, and initially these basic facts are reason enough to gravitate towards people you'd otherwise avoid like the plague.

I vaguely recognised a girl on my first day at the toddler group. Over time she's sort of latched on to me and it isn't until now that I realise we were vague acquaintances of old.

Well, that was enough. 'You must come round for lunch,' she says.

Of course, it's a disaster. Not only does she say grace – and no, that's not the name of her child – before she starts eating, but she seems to have some major issues with men. It turns out that, just after her baby was born, her husband inherited quite a lot of money.

'That's good,' I say enthusiastically.

'No, it's not,' she explains. 'He left me.'

'Right.'

'Taking the money with him. He now lives in Spain with his new girlfriend,' she goes on.

I try in vain to change the subject on a dozen occasions, but fail. Having spent an hour in her company, I almost feel like writing him a letter of sympathy.

18 May

Holiday attempt with small child no. 2.

Off to Ireland. The Irish love kids and the last time we were here we found Bone Dog. We leave the old soul back in Edinburgh this time but we revisit the wonderful Connemara coast where he was brought back to life by James, the local vet. We're booked into Rockglen, a lovely hotel, so we motor all the way with Louis in the back, gurgling, talking, singing and staring out the window. As we travel, we talk.

'I love the Irish,' I say. 'I want to come back as an Irish person.'

Dave agrees, with one exception. 'I can't stand that bloke who used to do *Game for a Laugh*. You know the guy,' he says. 'Is it Matthew Kelly?'

'No, he's not Irish!' I screech. 'You're thinking about Henry something . . . eh . . . *Henry* Kelly! He's on Classic FM and did that *Going for Gold* game show.' And we sing the theme tune as we pull up outside the hotel.

On arrival, we release Louis from his car seat and let him rumble around on the grass. We order tea and sandwiches and sit outside watching him explore his new surroundings whilst admiring the glorious view.

There are also glorious Irish accents all around us. I notice there's a balcony right above and, when I look up, I can't believe my eyes. For there, standing looking out over the same view as we are, is none other than Henry Kelly!

I tell Dave not to panic but to look up at the balcony above his head where he'll see the man himself. David just rolls his eyes disbelievingly and has another sandwich. He's lived with me too long.

Henry soon disappears back into his room and so it's not till later on, when we're chasing Louis around the garden and waiting for him to look sleepy, that a very buoyant Mr Kelly bounds over and says, 'What a lovely baby! Now what would his name be?'

I have to answer, as David's jaw is hanging loose. That'll teach him.

19 May

Our anniversary. What a lovely day we have, helped hugely by two factors: the Irish are just wonderful with kids, and Louis slept brilliantly last night. I feel human. David feels human. We're loving life. The top of the morning to you!

20 May

Why does this always happen to us? Last night we got Louis all tucked up and into bed, he went straight to sleep and David and I went downstairs for a nice, romantic dinner for two. Huh! Straight after dinner we head to the bar, where Mary – the piano player – is entertaining people. We join in the throng and have several more drinks. Eventually I end up on the piano, whilst David holds court at the bar with a selection of other guests – one of them being Henry Kelly. He's now not 'that irritating Irishman' but 'Henry – new friend. A really nice guy, actually'. Tee-hee! This gives me endless fodder for taking the mick – which I duly do.

Feel rough as hell this morning, though, so we sit in the garden and let Louis thump about with his cars. Thank goodness he's happy just toddling round.

24 May

Each morning we sit Louis in his high-chair, and he smiles and says 'Hello!' to everyone who comes into the diningroom as he splurts porridge and toast out of his mouth. He's a sunny, smiley child who seems very perceptive. I say this because there's a priest staying here too who's apparently quite high up in the Church. When he wanders into the diningroom of a morning, Louis looks him directly in the eye, sits up straight and, with no smile, gives him a very formal 'Good morning'. It cracks me up every time. Oh, how David and Henry will laugh about that later.

The rugby's on at the moment and the Irish are doing OK. David spends the afternoon watching a match in the priest's bedroom.

'Henry'll get jealous,' I warn him. He just ignores me.

26 May

Louis's talking gobbledy-gook constantly. His waking hours are now a constant hum of 'gaas' and 'goos'. He points into the sky as a bird flies over. 'Goo,' he says meaningfully. He strokes the hotel cat. 'Gaa,' he says sweetly. He chases the wee dog, Tiggy, falling flat on his face. 'Gummm,' he manages. He's noticing everything for the first time. And it's as if we're looking at everything in the world for the first time too. 'Look!' I say, pointing at this and that. 'Look!' David exclaims, pointing at everything else. We constantly point things out to him and, if it's not David, it's me pointing and shouting, 'Look!'

28 May

We're leaving today and, as we're saying our fond farewells to the people who run the hotel, one of the waiters who we've got to know well comes over and says to Louis, 'This is for you, Luke,' handing over a knitted doll. For a moment I'm puzzled, and then the penny drops. Every time Eamonn has seen us over the past week, we've been pointing and shouting 'look' – to the extent that he thinks this is Louis's actual name. We have a good laugh, break the news to him that our child is called Louis and depart. Back to reality.

29 May

That was a real holiday. The first we've had since Louis was born. We had good sleep, long lies and lots of fresh air. Return refreshed and ready for action. Ta-da!

3 June

So the perfect Brown Owl is in deep distress. It seems her precious, older child – older children are only allowed along to

the toddler group when on school holiday and if they're hers –
has brought some other little unannounced friends with him.
Namely nits.

Nits. Now there's a thing. Never had them before. But they're
all over the place. Nits. Gads! Am told only clean-haired children
get them. Yeh, right.

I look up nits on a website . . . Start the delousing process.

5 *June*
10 *stone* 12 *pounds*

Think Louis is now nit-free. Revolting little things. Just as I
collapse into bed and am lying there about to go to sleep, David
leaps out at speed, screeching.

'What in God's name is wrong with you?' I ask.

'Nits!' he says, pointing at my head. God, I've got them now. Joy.

7 *June*

Have to keep Louis away from other kids till the nits have died.
His have all gone. Mine, on the other hand, are having a ball.
There they all are, barely visible to the human eye, having sex,
holidaying and enjoying a great quality of life on my bloody head.

Phone hairdresser Derek. 'Can I get all my hair cut off, please?'

'No,' he replies and, in a voice I haven't heard him using
before – i.e. serious and mature – he says with all the gravitas of
an undertaker meeting a prospective client, 'I never cut a
woman's hair who has a small baby.'

'Why not?' I ask, incredulously.

''Cos their hormones are all over the place,' he explains, 'and
the chances are, two days after they've left the salon, kissing me
and telling me how much they love me, they'll phone me up
threatening to kill me, sue me and maim me 'cos I cut their hair
off – following their instructions in the first place.'

After I've threatened to kill him, sue him and maim him and slammed down the phone, I realise that perhaps, in this case, his is the voice of reason.

9 June

Am highly embarrassed to be infested with beasties. Due to the fact that my hair is long, it's proving harder to kill the little blighters off.

Going a little stir crazy. Try to keep the wee man amused. I wonder what my parents did without videos? Must have been Hell. We used to get *Watch with Mother* for fifteen minutes a day and revel in *Bill and Ben* – the original – and *Pogles Wood* and that would be it. Now it's such an easy option to plop said child in front of the TV and put on a vid.

Louis loves Barney, the great purple dinosaur. I know it's not for adults, but I still can't abide the thing. He sings and speaks in the most irritating voice, but Louis claps his hands together with glee and sits glued to the screen. Fine. Who am I to argue?

Dave thinks I've an unreasonable hatred for Barney because many years ago my friend Dynamite and I decided, when unemployed in London, to start our own children's entertainment company. We designed a poster and put it in all the shops and bars round Clapham, but no one phoned us. Ever. If only someone had, then I secretly believe we could have been that purple dinosaur Barney, irritating people the length and breadth of the globe from our Caribbean island in the sun. Yes, annoyingly, David is right. I may have issues.

10 June

Am almost nit-free. I still have a few gambolling around on my bonce, but, regardless, I head back to work – with my own headphones, just in case. Decide to avoid the subject in case the boss starts ringing a bell outside the studio shouting, 'Unclean!' I had no idea having children would mean I'd meet so many nice new friends. It's just a shame most of them live on my head!

18 June

In the park with Louis today. We're feeding the ducks. The water is not particularly clean and I'm dreaming idly of moving to the country and living a Felicity Kendall-*Good-Life*-type life.

As he throws some bread at a duck, it takes umbrage and flies off.

'Ducks fly!' he shouts in a state of shock. He didn't know that ducks flew. He just saw them all smogged up and pissed off on the pond in the park and it never occurred to him that they could do anything other than bob about among the tin cans and floating crisp packets. Feel guilty about bringing him up in a city.

21 June

Round to see cousin Amy and meet new cousin, Hugh. Just born. Kirsty looks calm.

We leave Amy and Louis in Amy's room playing as we coo over the new baby. When I go to retrieve my wee man to take him home, they're both completely naked under her bed. A new trick. Naked wee man.

25 June

Louis is standing in the bath tonight when he suddenly starts screeching.

'What's up?' I ask.

'Aaargh! What's that?' He holds out his hand in which he's resting his testicles – not having noticed them before.

'They're you're testicles,' I say, not knowing what else to say. I try to tell him that they're supposed to be there, and he's soon back to splashing about with his bubble bath and rubber duck.

26 June

David bathes Louis tonight and comes out of the bathroom creased up.

'What is it?' I ask.

'Louis was just showing me his tickles,' he manages, before continuing his helpless laugher.

28 June

David's birthday. I buy a lovely, big, gooey, chocolate cake and get Louis to toddle in holding it as we sing 'Happy Birthday'. The second David blows out the candles, Louis just launches his head forward and takes a great big bite right out of the side of it. My genes. I've always wanted to do that.

7 July
10 stone 10 pounds

Out for dinner tonight and when we get back there's a phone call from David's cousin, Stewart, in Canada. He's getting married in September and asks us to go over for the wedding. In a moment of madness and through an alcoholic haze we say yes.

There are only a few obstacles in our way: a) we have no money to go; b) we have no time to go; and c) we have to take Louis with us 'cos I'm not leaving him behind. Apart from that, it'll be great.

12 July

Go round to play with Louis's pals. I leave him there while I go off to a voice-over. By the time I come back, my friend's barring the door.

'Don't panic, but they've been playing a new game,' she explains. Hardly the best way to keep me calm and collected. But I can't help smiling when I walk in and realise that, not only have they stripped completely naked, but they've been playing 'tattoo Louis'. He's covered from top to toe in marker pen. There's barely an inch of skin that's not got a mark on it. A living monument to the Stabilo Boss.

Take him home and, before I put him in the bath, I show him to David. We consider getting someone to come round and do a family photograph to make into a Christmas card. Last year we received a card which featured a lovely group of well-groomed and beautiful children, all crowding around the piano as their proud parents looked on. Yes, this would pretty much sum us up. Fraught parents – tattooed child.

14 July

This whole MMR thing is not an exact science and we've been in a dilemma as to what on earth to do. We considered getting three single injections, but after much soul-searching, talking and reading, we're going to go ahead with it. The newspapers have been writing about the actual diseases that the injection immunises against – which are horrific. Measles, mumps and rubella.

David agrees to take Louis to the doctor as I'm convinced he can spot fear in my eyes. It all goes without a hitch and we're told that if there is a reaction, it'll be in about ten days.

24 July

No reaction to the MMR. Louis, it seems, is OK. Thank God.

18 August

10 stone 7 pounds

Haven't written an entry for ages. Life just seems to be whirling on. Louis grows, talks and is a laugh a minute. He's taken to Hoovering, which is fabulous. I've always had a real resistance to the '50s' housewife behaviour of old so, with a bit of luck, this little pudding will end up inadvertently keeping house. Wonderful. May consider getting him a Dyson for his birthday.

21 August

Friends coming to stay with their little baby so we think this is a good excuse to move Louis into a big bed. He's thrilled at the thought of being a big boy and not being behind bars.

7.30 p.m.

We go through the usual routine but, instead of the cot, we put him in his bed. He gets out of it about twenty-three times, by which point I'm about to throw in the towel. But Dave talks me round and, just as we're both hitting exasperation point, he stops reappearing. Success!

10.30 p.m.

Go in to check him before I go to bed. There he is, lying on the floor, with his ga-ga and his Tigger, sound asleep. I lift him up and tuck him in. Big boy in his bed. Tear to a glass eye.

14 September
10 stone 4 pounds

Long-haul flight to Canada, which I've been dreading. Two hours to Spain was bad enough, and since then we've avoided flying.

I went to the doctor and explained the previous experience with such drama that he handed over some cough mixture that'll knock the wee man out for most of the flight. Great. Asked him if I could have some too. He laughed. I wasn't bloody joking.

So, off we go to Canada to Dave's cousin Stewart's wedding. Yippee! Louis sleeps most of the way. Hurrah! A great flight.

Arrive in the pouring rain. Toronto looks great, but we're speeding – and when I say 'speeding', I mean speeding through the sheets of rain. At the helm of the car is Dave's aunt, Anne, who's intent on driving along in this pelting rain whilst chatting to us. We're very grateful that she's collected us, but I really wish she wouldn't insist on looking at us in the back seat while she talks.

Eventually, in a very high-pitched voice, I say, 'Please slow down, I think I'm going to be sick!' Sick as parrot to get all the way to Toronto only to be obliterated in a car accident – I neglect to add.

It's late evening when we arrive but, as Louis has slept during the flight, the last thing he wants to do is put his head down. So I spend the first night in Toronto staring out at the rainy Canadian outback playing with cars.

15 September
6 a.m.

Fall into a slump at the same time as Louis.

9.30 a.m.

'The wedding's taking place up north. Why don't you borrow my car?' Dave's aunt offers generously.

We accept and both envision ourselves speeding through the Canadian countryside in the Volvo estate we nearly died in yesterday. Perfect. We arrange to set off tomorrow morning.

16–18 September

As we pack our bags again and stand outside after breakfast saying our farewells, Dave's aunt hands over the keys to the car – not her husband's Volvo but – oh no! – her Datsun Cherry, which is older than I am. Thanks, we smile, as we clamber in and begin our journey.

And what a journey. There are distances in this country that we can only ever imagine. Apparently, they drive as far as the length of Britain just for dinner – a gruelling enough prospect without the fact that this car only goes 55 m.p.h. It doesn't need to go any faster, though, as the speed limit's 55 m.p.h. It's four days to the wedding. I don't know if we'll make it.

I map-read and Dave drives. The map-reading is a waste of time. It's just one long, straight road from Toronto to f***ing nowhere. We stop and get out occasionally to shout at each other out of earshot of Louis, who talks in the back the whole time. Initially we're enthused and look out over the barren, flat landscape or let Louis have a wee toddle about. But frankly the road is long and straight and dull. Every town is an exact clone of the one before. The bigger ones offer a Dunkin Donut, a McDonald's and a selection of other chain stores before hitting the motel line, which is where things get interest-ing. Here we briefly play Russian roulette and pick one we think will be OK for the night.

They're all small, cardboard hutches with no character, no charm and, without exception, no sound-proofing. The antics of some of the people we stay next to at least raise a smile as we lie there, feet hanging over the bottom of the bed, cursing the day we answered the phone half-cut back in July and accepted this invitation.

Making a gross generalisation, I'd say the smaller towns tend to lack imagination. The first street we see is called First Street, the last street as we leave the built-up area is called Last Street. The winters must be so damn cold in these parts that people's brains have frozen. This is not how I imagined Canada to be at all.

19 September

After three days and three nights of endless, mindless, excrutiatingly dull driving, we arrive in Souix St Marie, the venue for the nuptials. Everyone else has flown in and so looks relaxed, happy and ready to party.

We're introduced as the family from Scotland, grey-faced, exhausted and grumpy – just how you'd imagine a family from Scotland to be. The only things missing are the very red hair and the kilts. The kilt will make an appearance tomorrow, but for now we check into the hotel.

The thought of a hot bath and a lie-down in a clean bed cheers me up big time. Smiling and laughing for the first time in a few days, we chase Louis down the corridor towards our room as the porter tells us we have the last beds available in town. With this piece of information, he duly opens the door.

The smell sort of hits us in the face, as it's immediately obvious we're now in some sort of flood situation. A large pipe is spewing out what to the untrained eye looks like shit all over the carpet. With a sinking feeling, we call the manager to complain. He's sympathetic whilst telling us there're no other rooms available in the hotel. So it's the cesspit or nothing. We toss a coin. The Datsun Cherry or the plague. It's a tough call, but having sat upright in the bloody Datsun for what feels like a lifetime, we plump for risking dysentery.

Another phone call and we beg dozens of bin-liners from the over-stretched staff and spend the evening barricading our bedroom from the effluence. Service industry? Huh! I'm telling you, this lot could give the Scottish Tourist Board a run for its money.

20 September

The wedding. The bride, Maria, is a gorgeous Italian, and Stewart is the Scottish groom in a kilt. Everything's going swimmingly.

It's going to be a long ceremony as it's a Catholic service. Expecting this, I've uncharacteristically stuffed my handbag with goodies so as to bribe Louis to 'Sssh!'

As it gets to the quiet bit halfway through the ceremony, perhaps it's the surfeit of E-numbers that kicks in but, for no apparent reason, Louis suddenly bucks his whole body backwards. This causes me to lose grip of him and, in slow motion, his head then comes smashing down on the wooden pew in front. There's a sickening, dull thud and then nothing. I look at his face, which is going from normal pink to deep crimson. His mouth is open, his eyes are tightly shut and he's brewing up a monumental screech. I must take action – must get along the pew and attempt to make a run for the door. I quickly gather him up in my arms. I know that when this little beauty blows, he's going to drown out everyone and everything and sound like he's being murdered.

Just as I get to my feet, the noise is unleashed. A remarkably high-pitched, blood-curdling scream, the like of which I haven't heared since watching *American Werewolf in London* in the '80s. It brings everyone and everything to a shuddering halt. Harassed beyond belief, I smile as best I can whilst barging past the people in our row until eventually, under the eye of the whole congregation, I burst out the back door and start putting my wee boy back together again.

After fifteen minutes he's dried, de-snotted and calm – which is how he'll remain till he clocks the great big bruise on the front of his head later on. 'Egg' doesn't go halfway to describing it.

Everything else is great, though, and we're so glad we made the trip. Everyone's lovely and meeting all Dave's Canadian/ Scottish relatives makes the traumatic journey worthwhile. Whether or not Louis has amnesia, we'll have to wait and see. In some ways, if he can block out the three-day journey up here, it might be a blessing.

21–24 September

On our way back to Toronto in the Datsun, we check into a hotel that one of the wedding guests recommended. It's lovely and has a pool.

As we're taking stock, lying back and relaxing, we watch as Louis wanders towards the water . . . and then just keeps walking into it like it's an extension of the side of the pool. It's Buster Keaton without the funny ending. The wee man and his egg-head sink like a stone. My heart bursts. Dave jumps in to retrieve him. Louis blubbers hysterically, I join in, the barman brings me a large drink, I drain it. After a refill, my heart returns to normal.

Sit eagle-eyed staring at Louis for the rest of the time in case we get a repeat performance. So far Buster has left the building. Phew!

We survive the rest of the car trip back and are keen to get to the airport in good time so as to check in for our return journey and get seats together. It seems we are nice and early – twenty-four hours, to be precise. God. We've said farewell to family and friends and are now stranded here. A quick call secures us a hotel room and off we go to explore down-town

Toronto. We see the CNN Tower and take a car around some of the sights. It's lovely, but just beam me up, Scottie. I want to go home.

4 October
11 a.m.

Swallowing stuff. Leave him for a moment while I go on my daily hunt for the walk-about phone. When I return he looks different. His face is flushed and he's squinting at his Lego. *Oh – my – God!* I think he's swallowed a bit.

12.30 p.m.

Find a piece of Lego in Louis's nappy. He hadn't swallowed it, it seems, but, for some peculiar reason, just jammed it into his pants. Thank God! In between times I speak to my sage old friend Fiona, who has loads of kids and always manages to calm me down in times of unreasonable anxiety.

She surprises me when she says, quite adamantly, 'For God's sake, don't let your son do that!'

'Oh God!' I reply. 'Why not? Will he die?'

'No,' she says. 'It's bloody expensive!' The voice of reason.

Two years old!

13 November
10 stone 2 pounds

Louis's second birthday.

He absolutely *loves* Noddy. Why? I don't know. To me, Noddy is in the same ballpark of annoyance as Barney, the blasted purple dinosaur. It may have something to do with the fact that the stories only have one Scottish character – a sneaky thief – and that, to add insult to injury, whoever produced the series didn't even have the sense to hire a real Scot to do the voice-over. So, the token Scottish crook is played by an English actor who sounds bloody ridiculous trying to sound like he's from north of the Border. Perhaps I'm being pedantic, and David tells me to stop trying to explain it to Louis because he just looks confused.

So I bite the bullet, swallow my prejudice and hire a Noddy costume for David. We'll see how fond he is of our little friend after this, I say to him, as he runs off along the road – giant foam suit in hand – so as to get changed in the car and surprise the kids.

Meanwhile, all the wee toddle-bags are stumbling round, eating crisps and dancing to *The Singing Kettle*. Looking out the window and seeing Dave lolloping along the street dressed as Noddy gives my pelvic floor another wake-up call. Get myself together in time for him to ring the bell.

'Oh, I wonder who this is?' I say in my overexcited BBC children's presenter voice. Right on cue and like the Pied Piper, all the wee ones follow me to the door. I open it and, before I can say, 'Look, everyone, it's Noddy!', there are a series of blood-curdling screams and the thundering of little hooves as all the wee toots run as fast as they can for cover, crying hysterically. To say that they're petrified of the 6-foot Noddy would be like saying Telly Savalas was not that hairy. They're beside themselves. The wave of hysteria hits a crescendo as I stand there helplessly, the sound and smell of nappies being filled permeating the atmosphere.

Dave – a.k.a. Noddy – is immediately dispatched back to the car as we try to calm everyone down. Most go home, snottering and snivelling and, I'm fairly convinced, emotionally disturbed.

6.30 p.m.

After the mayhem subsides, we try to unravel how it had all gone so terribly wrong. We come to the conclusion that Noddy

looks about 6 inches tall on TV, so all the toddlers would probably expect him to be a tiny, wee, pocket-sized Tom Thumb.
Then Gigantor appears, waving and wobbling around, and no
wonder they're petrified. Bloody funny, though.

2.30 a.m.
Still laughing about it when I wake up in the middle of the night.

3 December
10 *stone*

So potty-training is the next fun thing we have to tackle. The
nursery I've ear-marked for Louis will only take him if he's out
of nappies. This is an incentive. Girls, apparently, do it earlier
and easier than boys, but I decide to make an effort and start
him today. I buy a plastic potty.

God, where are you supposed to start? Nappy off, I watch
him like a hawk so that as soon as he looks as though he needs
to go, I take his hand and run towards the potty. During the
course of the day we make it more times than not. A good start.

5 December
A great deal of my day is spent watching Louis sitting – smiling
and bare-bottomed – on the pot. When occasionally he does
something, I leap to my feet, clapping and cheering. No, this
isn't going to be traumatic.

8 December
Find a poo on the carpet today. A human one. So I don't think
he's quite got the hang of it yet. He's piddling like a good 'un
in the potty, though.

Am told a very funny story about a friend whose son is at the same stage. She and her husband, Peter, had friends round for supper – people without children. As they settled down for dinner, wee Hamish came wombling through carrying a plate on which sat a beautifully formed turd – his. He was delighted and I dare say looking for a rather different reaction from the one he actually got.

18 December

I can't believe it's Christmas again. This year the lights are on, the eggnog is slipping down a treat, the tree is twinkling and Louis has even helped me decorate it – despite the fact that every single decoration he hangs is on the same branch. Suddenly my loyalty to New Year has slipped and Christmas is definitely my thing. Watching the little boy birling around in amongst the boxes under the tree is hilarious.

25 December

It takes Louis an hour to open his stocking. Every little thing is a joy – be it a plastic penguin or a chocolate mouse. I've never seen anyone so ecstatic in my life. And when he realises there'll be another gift for him downstairs under the tree, I think he's going to burst with excitement.

After clambering downstairs, Louis opens it up – a sit-on digger. Squeals with delight, ignores the digger and promptly climbs into the box to play. Typical!

This all overshadows the strange, metal, World War Two warden's helmet Dave gives me – the mother of his child – for Christmas. I assume it's one of those 'seemed-like-a-good-idea-at-the-time' things. Funny bloke.

Even manage to cook a turkey this year. Admittedly, I do leave the giblets in by mistake, but it does have a lovely, gamy flavour and, when I eventually confess my mistake, everyone declares that it's so delicious, the next time they cook a turkey they'll leave the giblets in too. Could be the drink talking. Still.

31 December

Mum and Dad say they'll baby-sit. Yahoo! We meet up with friends for dinner and a great time.

11.45 p.m.

Torn between going to Princes Street for midnight or heading home. We have a choice. We have baby-sitters. Choose to go home and toast the New Year with Mum and Dad – a.k.a. Grandma and Grandpa. I have a good feeling about this coming year, I really do.

9 April

Haven't had even a minute to write my diary lately. Life and my baggy bits seem to be on an even keel at the moment and, although life will never be the same again, I wouldn't change a thing.

I'm more aware of time passing since Louis arrived. I notice Christmases and birthdays so much more. It really makes me realise how fast it all goes by and – unbelievably, it seems – my little pudding starts nursery today.

He has a blue overall with his name on it and a little plastic box for his lunch. I get him up and off we go. He trots in without so much as a backward glance. When he's introduced to the other kids, he clings briefly on to my legs, but as soon as he spots another wee boy zooming some cars around, he's off.

I wave goodbye and then stand in the garden and watch through the window for a while as he bumbles around, chatting to people and staring at the goldfish. Within three minutes he's wearing a fireman's hat and giggling.

It's his first step on the road to independence and, as I walk back to the car and get in, I know that it's my first real step to reclaiming mine too. Before starting the engine I reflect on the great adventure. I know hormones play tricks . . . babies look cute again . . . And as the fruit of my loins goes off into the big, wide world, I wonder if I'll do it again. The choice: a) flick back to p. 1 and start over; or b) get a puppy.

Whatever the decision, with a lump in my throat I know that for me – at least for now – the nappy years are over.

(By the way, 9 stone 12 pounds and holding!)

List of 'vital' equipment bought for baby before birth

Car seat

Moses basket with stand and ridiculous, long, frilly cover thing, plus sheets and blankets to fit

Three-in-one pram (cot, buggy and pram)

Endless supply of soft, dangly toys to keep baby amused whilst in pram

Net to put over pram to stop cats getting baby. (Don't actually have cats, but you can never be too careful)

Huge and hideous changing bag in same pattern as pram

Big cot that turns into a bed at a later stage, giving three sleeping possibilities

Changing table

Changing mat

Plastic box to keep nappy bags and Sudocreme in

Nappy dispenser

Nappy disposal unit

Baby bath

Bath thermometer

Realistic list of equipment required for first six months

Car seat

Buggy

Cot

Realistic assessment of other items purchased

Moses basket – *see* our bed, in which he slept due to worry that too many frills might suffocate him

Three-in-one pram – a wee buggy for £25 from Mothercare would've done the job

Net to put over pram – redundant for a woman with a dog who has a pathological hatred of cats

Hideous changing bag – any old bag would've done and preferably one that wasn't big and frilly with blue polka-dots

Changing table – *see* any available flat surface

Changing mat – *see* above

Plastic box to keep nappy bags etc. in – *see* utter waste of time

Nappy dispenser – *see* plastic bags they're sold in

Nappy disposal unit – *see* bin

Baby bath – *see* sink

Bath thermometer – *see* elbow

Total amount out of pocket?

Let's not go there. Too upsetting.